# **PALGRAVE** Studies in Oral History

## Series Editors: Linda Shopes and Bruce M. Stave

### Editorial Board

**Rina Benmayor**
Division of Humanities and Communication &
Oral History and Community Memory Archive
California State University Monterey Bay
United States

**Indira Chowdhury**
Archival Resources for Contemporary History
India

**Pilar Dominguez**
Department of Historical Sciences
Division of Political Thought and Social Movements
Las Palmas de Gran Canaria
Universidad de Las Palmas de Gran Canaria
España

**Sean Field**
Centre for Popular Memory
Department of Historical Studies
University of Cape Town
South Africa

**Alexander Freund**
Department of History &
Oral History Centre
University of Winnipeg
Canada

**Anna Green**
College of Humanities
University of Exeter
United Kingdom

**Paula Hamilton**
Faculty of Humanities & Social Sciences &
Australian Centre for Public History
University of Technology Sydney
Australia

**Paul Ortiz**
Department of History & Samuel Proctor Oral
History Program
University of Florida
United States

*The Order Has Been Carried Out: History, Memory, and Meaning of a Nazi Massacre in Rome*, by Alessandro Portelli (2003)

*Sticking to the Union: An Oral History of the Life and Times of Julia Ruuttila*, by Sandy Polishuk (2003)

*To Wear the Dust of War: From Bialystok to Shanghai to the Promised Land, an Oral History*, by Samuel Iwry, edited by L. J. H. Kelley (2004)

*Education as My Agenda: Gertrude Williams, Race, and the Baltimore Public Schools*, by Jo Ann Robinson (2005)

*Remembering: Oral History Performance*, edited by Della Pollock (2005)

*Postmemories of Terror: A New Generation Copes with the Legacy of the "Dirty War,"* by Susana Kaiser (2005)

*Growing Up in the People's Republic: Conversations between Two Daughters of China's Revolution*, by Ye Weili and Ma Xiaodong (2005)

*Life and Death in the Delta: African American Narratives of Violence, Resilience, and Social Change*, by Kim Lacy Rogers (2006)

*Creating Choice: A Community Responds to the Need for Abortion and Birth Control, 1961–1973*, by David P. Cline (2006)

*Voices from This Long Brown Land: Oral Recollections of Owens Valley Lives and Manzanar Pasts*, by Jane Wehrey (2006)

*Radicals, Rhetoric, and the War: The University of Nevada in the Wake of Kent State*, by Brad E. Lucas (2006)

*The Unquiet Nisei: An Oral History of the Life of Sue Kunitomi Embrey*, by Diana Meyers Bahr (2007)

*Sisters in the Brotherhoods: Working Women Organizing for Equality in New York City*, by Jane LaTour (2008)

*Iraq's Last Jews: Stories of Daily Life, Upheaval, and Escape from Modern Babylon*, edited by Tamar Morad, Dennis Shasha, and Robert Shasha (2008)

*Soldiers and Citizens: An Oral History of Operation Iraqi Freedom from the Battlefield to the Pentagon*, by Carl Mirra (2008)

*Overcoming Katrina: African American Voices from the Crescent City and Beyond*, by D'Ann R. Penner and Keith C. Ferdinand (2009)

*Bringing Desegregation Home: Memories of the Struggle toward School Integration in Rural North Carolina*, by Kate Willink (2009)

*I Saw It Coming: Worker Narratives of Plant Closings and Job Loss*, by Tracy E. K'Meyer and Joy L. Hart (2010)

*Speaking History: Oral Histories of the American Past, 1865–Present*, by Sue Armitage and Laurie Mercier (2010)

*Surviving Bhopal: Dancing Bodies, Written Texts, and Oral Testimonials of Women in the Wake of an Industrial Disaster*, by Suroopa Mukherjee (2010)

*Living with Jim Crow: African American Women and Memories of the Segregated South*, by Anne Valk and Leslie Brown (2010)

*Gulag Voices: Oral Histories of Soviet Incarceration and Exile*, by Jehanne M. Gheith and Katherine R. Jolluck (2011)

*Detained without Cause: Muslims' Stories of Detention and Deportation in America after 9/11*, by Irum Shiekh (2011)

*Soviet Communal Living: An Oral History of the Kommunalka*, by Paola Messana (2011)

*Oral History and Photography*, edited by Alexander Freund and Alistair Thomson (2011)

*Memories of Queer Latino San Francisco*, by Horacio N. Roque-Ramirez (2011)

# Soviet Communal Living

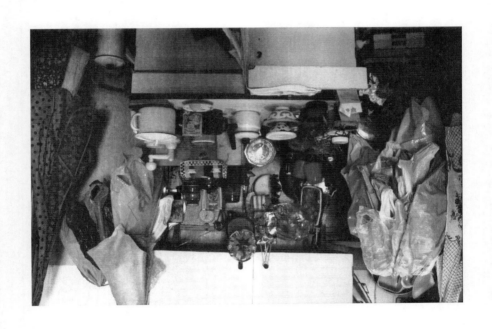

# Soviet Communal Living

## An Oral History of the Kommunalka

Paola Messana

SOVIET COMMUNAL LIVING
Copyright © Paola Messana, 2011.

All rights reserved.

First published in 2011 by
PALGRAVE MACMILLAN®
in the United States—a division of St. Martin's Press LLC,
175 Fifth Avenue, New York, NY 10010.

Where this book is distributed in the UK, Europe and the rest of the world,
this is by Palgrave Macmillan, a division of Macmillan Publishers Limited,
registered in England, company number 785998, of Houndmills,
Basingstoke, Hampshire RG21 6XS.

Palgrave Macmillan is the global academic imprint of the above companies
and has companies and representatives throughout the world.

Palgrave® and Macmillan® are registered trademarks in the United States,
the United Kingdom, Europe and other countries.

ISBN: 978–0–230–11016–8

Library of Congress Cataloging-in-Publication Data is available from the
Library of Congress.

Saint Petersburg, 2002, Plastic bags in a kitchen, "Kommunalki," © Françoise
Huguier

A catalogue record of the book is available from the British Library.

Design by Newgen Imaging Systems (P) Ltd., Chennai, India.

First edition: March 2011

10 9 8 7 6 5 4 3 2 1

Printed and bound in Great Britain by
CPI Antony Rowe , Chippenham and Eastbourne

# Contents

| | |
|---|---|
| *Series Editors' Foreword* | xi |
| *Foreword* by *Vasily Rudich* | xiii |
| Introduction | 1 |
| **CHAPTER 1** "Uplotnienie": Filling Up | 7 |
| **CHAPTER 2** White Army, Red Army | 11 |
| **CHAPTER 3** The Visit to Lenin | 15 |
| **CHAPTER 4** Like Life in Naples | 19 |
| **CHAPTER 5** I, Princess Golitsyn | 23 |
| **CHAPTER 6** Spy Stories | 25 |
| **CHAPTER 7** The Black Crow | 31 |
| **CHAPTER 8** Even the Baltics | 33 |
| **CHAPTER 9** The Siege of Leningrad | 39 |
| **CHAPTER 10** The Denunciation | 43 |

**viii** / Contents

## CHAPTER 11
Summer 1948                                                    49

## CHAPTER 12
The Ambulance, the Dead, and the Others                        53

## CHAPTER 13
The American Legacy                                            57

## CHAPTER 14
Jewish Poison in the Pots                                      61

## CHAPTER 15
The Letter                                                    67

## CHAPTER 16
New Year's Eve Celebration                                    71

## CHAPTER 17
How Thirty People Can Share an Apartment                      75

## CHAPTER 18
The Gulag and the Roslovian Smell                             79

## CHAPTER 19
Ballad of a Soldier                                           87

## CHAPTER 20
Lenins, Nothing But Lenins                                    93

## CHAPTER 21
Dissidence                                                    97

## CHAPTER 22
The Passageway Room                                          103

## CHAPTER 23
The Prostitute                                               107

## CHAPTER 24
The French Lover                                             111

## CHAPTER 25
Masha L. and the Spirit of the Kommunalka                    115

## CHAPTER 26
The English Girl and the Blackmarketeer                      123

**CHAPTER 27**
   An Officer in the Strategic Nuclear Forces                       129
**CHAPTER 28**
   From Putsch to Putsch                                            135
**CHAPTER 29**
   Seventeen Years after the Fall of the USSR                       139
**CHAPTER 30**
   Two Sisters through History                                      143

*Appendix A*                                                         145
*Appendix B*                                                         147
*Appendix C*                                                         149
*Appendix D*                                                         151
*Notes*                                                              157

## Series Editors' Foreword

In George Orwell's dystopian novel, *1984*, people suffered constant surveillance. Big Brother was always watching, and no one could be trusted not to spy on a "friend." In telling the story of Soviet Russia's *Kommunalka* or communal apartments, Paola Messana limns a portrait of real life communal living in the USSR. In the aftermath of the 1917 Bolshevik Revolution, with housing scarce and an ideology that promoted the elimination of class distinctions, the wealthy and middle classes found their housing units expropriated so that apartments that originally housed one family became home to many. Large, previously privileged, families resided in a single room with other rooms crammed with strangers, often strangers with whom they had little in common and with whom they never would have associated. They shared kitchens and what there were of bathrooms. This allowed the authorities to play tenant off against tenant and intensify surveillance. As one of the interviewees in the following pages remarked, he was fortunate because "the inhabitants of our apartment were louts but not informers." The power of the narratives included in this volume stem from the stories they tell about daily life under difficult conditions. Paola Messana is a distinguished journalist, not an academic or public oral historian like so many other authors in this series. As such, her contribution is less about method and more about the interview process's ability to capture human interest and dramatize the everyday life that marked Soviet communal living; that experience resonates in collective memory to this day. Most of the interviews were conducted during the first half of the 1990s and reveal the power of oral history to open up to the world what had gone on behind the "iron curtain." The author granted anonymity where desired, which helped to break the imposed silence of the Soviet past. All these recollections come together to reveal a fascinating account of life under communism.

In doing so, this book joins another volume in the series about a significant facet of Soviet society, *Gulag Voices: Oral Histories of Soviet*

**xii / Series Editors' Foreword**

*Incarceration and Exile*, and it adds to its global scope that includes works on India, China, Iraq, Italy, and Argentina as well as a forthcoming contribution on South Africa. The Palgrave Studies in Oral History not only crosses geographic boundaries but also investigates a multitude of subjects and offers a variety of methodological approaches. Its creative authors bring oral history from the recorder and the archive to the printed page and breathe life into the telling of the past for the benefit of scholars, students, and the general reader.

Bruce M. Stave
University of Connecticut

Linda Shopes
Carlisle, Pennsylvania

# Foreword

Understanding a society and culture different from our own requires the possession of knowledge and exercise of imagination. Traditional scholarship may provide an interested reader with an array of data and analysis of a particular cultural context. It is, however, much less often than one would wish that an academic study might stimulate the reader's imagination.

In the course of the last three centuries the West often experienced difficulties in adequately responding to the events happening in that huge country called Russia. This was not necessarily caused by the lack of available information—rather, by the preponderance of sweeping generalizations and clichés, such as "traditional authoritarianism" or "mysterious Russian soul." None of this is, of course, helpful in understanding Russia's social and cultural environment or the mindset of Russian people: empathy is rooted in the capacity for imagination, which in turn relies on a multiplicity of details, and much less on any theoretical framework. As a consequence, many Western observers, ignoring the complexities of historical processes, preferred either to demonize pre-revolutionary Russia (which was far from an ideal society, but appears almost decent when compared with fascist or communist regimes), or—in the case of the European and American left—celebrate the alleged achievements of the Soviet Union.

Starting with Alexander Solzhenitsyn's *The Gulag Archipelago* and the subsequent flow of dissident publications, Western readers became better acquainted with many details of Soviet political life, such as the structure of authority, the penitentiary system, and the shadow economy. Occasionally, they could also glimpse the intricacies of social and interpersonal relations against the background of the Soviet daily life from reportage by Western journalists, who themselves were in the position of an outsider. Contemporary Russian fiction might have offered yet another opportunity for such insights, but only insofar as a few particular works did succeed in attracting public attention, such as Mikhail Bulgakov's *Master and Margarita* and Anatoly Rybakov's *Children of Arbat*, or the short stories of Tatyana Tolstaya. Much of that literature, some of it of considerable quality, remains untranslated or unappreciated.

As a result, the Western picture of life in the Soviet Union was (and still is) fraught with gaps, which accounts for the sense of bafflement on the part of many foreign visitors with regard to attitudes and behavior they observe in the Russians they meet. Even though the Soviet Union is now a thing of the past, it continues to cast a long shadow over those who happened to grow up under the communist regime. Thus a proper and thorough understanding of life in Soviet Russia not only is a matter of historical interest but directly pertains to Russia's present and future.

Paola Messana's *Soviet Communal Living* splendidly fills one especially glaring gap. It deals with a phenomenon most of the Westerners know, at best, only by hearsay. They find it difficult to imagine that several families, totally unknown to each other, could for many decades coexist within the limited space of the same apartment, compelled to do so not by poverty or other circumstances, but by government decree. This I know by experience: whenever I described to American friends the predicament of my own Leningrad youth (I lived in one room,with my aunt and grandmother, aged 90, in an apartment that with 6 more families, and 17 residents total), I was invariably met with expressions of disbelief. I needed to elaborate, adding further details and examples, and explaining that the same or similar conditions were shared, for the most part, even by people considered—by Soviet standards—well-to-do, before I had convinced at least some of my listeners.

This made me appreciate the difficulties that an individual testimony presents to an audience willing to sympathize but reluctant to look beyond the familiar. The power of Messana's book lies in the accumulation of such testimonies, meticulously selected and faithfully reproduced. In my view, the value of this book ultimately surpasses that of any sociological analysis, since it offers a succession of human dramas played out under circumstances that are often close to absurd, with the nuances of character and behavior close to incredible. This is extraordinarily rich material for any student not only of the Soviet era, but of human nature.

This effect owes also to the author's skill in preserving a variety of narrative voices. They belong to former aristocrats and members of the intelligentsia, soldiers and ordinary citizens, and even foreigners, who for whatever reasons found themselves living in the ambience of the kommunalka. Several stories offer special insights into the political and cultural history of the Soviet Union, such as the account of the daughter of Ivars Smilga, one of Lenin's close associates; the personal details of the famous Soviet spy Richard Sorge; the tribulations of the great movie director Grigori Chukhrai, whose struggle with hostility in the kommunalka forced him to write the script of his award-winning film "The Ballad of the Soldier" only at nights, in the bathroom; and the reminiscences of the son of the writer Yuli Daniel, whose arrest in 1965 and subsequent trial generated worldwide protest and proved largely responsible for the emergence of the human rights movement in the USSR.

The strategy chosen by Paola Messana permits the reader to experience the kommunalka from the perspective of an insider, with all the material hardships and moral traumas involved. One encounters a range of characters and types, some of them familiar, others less so—at times well-known figures within Soviet life, such as KGB informers, while at other times seemingly taken from a sensational Russian novel, like drunken murderers armed with a proverbial axe. The reader is plunged into a peculiar blend of solidarity and paranoia, with an apartment's residents fearing that their neighbors will try to poison them (or, at the very least, spit in their casseroles), while at the same time genuinely capable of enjoying each other's company, dancing together in their kitchen on New Year's Eve. This last point is not without merit: this communal coexistence, however perverse, helped to create strong human and emotional bonds, both negative and positive, even as so many people in the West acutely suffered from alienation. The narratives from this book provide, side by side with demonstrations of baseness or vulgarity, examples of courage and generosity that elsewhere might not have materialized. In other words, the phenomenon of the kommunalka entails a paradox: on the one hand, it makes understandable why the Russian language still lacks the word for privacy; and on the other, it is not impossible that the gift for close friendship that many Russians are very proud of may owe at least something to their being brought up and socialized in the narrow confines of a communal apartment.

The voices in the book differ in the quality of their narration. Some stories display high literacy and sophistication, with psychological or cultural commentary—and at times, one may even suspect, some artistic embellishment, although this is never a reason to deny their basic truth.

Many of the narrators are elderly, whose memories can seem somewhat confused, especially with regard to chronology. Other tales are simple, straightforward and entirely lucid. All of this, of course, is part and parcel of any "oral" or "living" history. Taken together, they demonstrate beyond doubt the vital importance of the kommunalka in the lives of Soviet citizens and explain why for most of them the "housing question" proved a greater concern during the years of the cold war than the arms race and the threat of nuclear confrontation.

All in all, Paola Messana's book makes fascinating reading for scholars as well as laymen: the former is given a wealth of empirical data further to ponder and analyze; the latter is introduced into a world bordering on the surreal that is, at the same time, as real as any, though an ordinary Westerner would hardly have imagined it even in a dream.

Vasily Rudich
Formerly Associate Professor of Classics
and History at Yale University
New Haven, September 2010

# Introduction

In April 1990, when I had just arrived in what was still the USSR, I met a woman aged around 50 at an auction in Moscow, an elegant Soviet Jewess, who had bought a rare Galle. She agreed to grant me an interview at her home on Lenin's Prospect. When I entered the apartment, she took me along a long dark corridor to a room, a real museum, where we sat down for the interview. I was astonished that she had crammed all these treasures into this room when the apartment seemed to me to be huge.

For more than an hour we discussed the wonders that she had collected over the years—imperial porcelain, extremely rare clocks and precious vases—when I asked her whether this fortune was insured for theft. I saw her turn pale, get up, and close the reinforced door.

With horror I then understood that the young man who I had seen upon arriving, and who I heard walking in the hallway, was not her son as I had thought but A NEIGHBOR. She confirmed this: "We live in a communal apartment."

The atmosphere emanating from the apartment was so peculiar that I decided to continue my investigation into the world of the "Kommunalka," or Communal Apartments. As I progressed in my research, in my encounters, I understood that the history of the USSR, its ideology, its people, that the human behavior which often overwhelms us was reflected in these apartments.

Imagine... imagine that all of a sudden the police or some other authority installs a family in your living room without warning, another in your dining room, a third in your children's bedroom. These intruders are total strangers to you; you no longer recognize the university professor, the bus driver, or the electrician who descend on you with furniture and baggage, they no longer even acknowledge each other.

Imagine that you find yourself from one day to the next confined to a single room that becomes your entire universe, where you have to eat your meals, read, listen to music or sleep, with your children or as the case may be your pets, and that from now on you are obliged to share the kitchen, bathroom, and toilet with these strangers. Not just for several weeks, but for decades or even your whole life, because in the USSR the "propiska" system, the enforced, obligatory registration to a residence, was prevalent.

A large majority of Soviets—there were 300 million in the beginning of the '90s—lived in these communal apartments. Big-name directors, famous actors, journalists, professors, writers, dissidents, policemen, lawyers, prosecutors, piano teachers, opera singers, musicians—knew the kommunalka. Other than high-up communists, there were few who escaped the collective apartment, where even KGB agents and spies were housed.

Up until the mid-1960s, 80 percent of the population in the cities were affected, from Moscow to Baku, from Leningrad (today once again called St. Petersburg) to Kiev, from Odessa now in Ukraine to Sverdlovsk (once again Ekaterinburg), the city of Boris Yeltsin and Roman Abramovich. Aware of the problem, Nikita Khrushchev had immense blocks of city residences built as individual apartments and reduced the proportion of kommunalki[1] to 50 percent, then to 30 percent.

The USSR collapsed in December 1991, but the kommunalka still made up close to 20 percent of the housing in Moscow, and much more in St. Petersburg. In the Russian capital, two years after the disappearance of the USSR, 1.5 million people still lived in communal apartments.

It was during these years that building developers took over the cities, and first and foremost, Moscow. Buying individual rooms for a song from those who had become their owners thanks to a 1992 decree of Boris Yeltsin, they privatized enormous communal apartments in the historic center, renovated them cheaply, and put them on the rental market, which started to grow exponentially. A housing boom still going strong, years later.

Some of these developers amassed fortunes in a very short period, and the number of communal apartments in Moscow shrank to almost nothing. But insofar as prices rose, kommunalki in the beginning of this new century were more and more difficult to privatize, either because one of the inhabitants refused or because of the increasing costs of buying out and renovating apartments in which everything needed to be redone. So, developers turned to building new construction on the city outskirts or in chic suburbs. That is how, while the majority of Muscovites think that they have disappeared, I found in 2008 several kommunalki, relics of a bygone era, true testaments of the past at a time when Moscow has become the city that holds after New York the world record number of billionaires.

The kommunalka became a true obsession for me, and I wanted to tell the story, chronologically, of the history of a country that haunted the twentieth century from the October Revolution to the collapse of the USSR and to today's Russia, through the narratives of the inhabitants of communal apartments.

The stories that I collected are varied. Sometimes, the kommunalka is at the center of the story, sometimes it is just the décor, sometimes it is only there as a barely discernable watermark. The stories are left as is; my speakers often overwhelmed me with their sense of the anecdote, of suspense, of details of daily life.

Almost all the apartments are identical; that's without a doubt what is the most striking, from Baku to Kiev, from Moscow to Novosibirsk. Even the indefinable smell of the entryway, a mixture of dust and dubious cleanliness, without the perfumes of all the Western cleansers, the same closed doors looking out onto a dark hallway, the same pile of boxes and old suitcases scattered everywhere, the same kitchens with lots of little cupboards, lots of little tables and at least two gas stoves, where each family has access to one burner of one stove, the same sordid bathrooms lit by a bare bulb, the same row of dismal laundry drying on individually distinct clotheslines depending on whether they belonged to one family or another.

I used many methods to find my eyewitnesses: my Russian friends, human rights organizations such as Memorial that keeps archival documents of Soviet dissidence, and above all, a research want ad placed in 1993 in two newspapers with a large circulation. The hundreds of calls that came day and night made me understand even better, if that were necessary, how much this problem still exists, if not in daily reality, at least in the collective memory. For almost two months, my telephone literally never stopped ringing; we had to unplug it at 1 a.m. to sleep a little, and the phone calls continued for another four months after the advertisements came out.

4 / Soviet Communal Living

In the mud, in the snow, in the rain, I visited dozens of these apartments, often scoring big, getting memorable research, mainly in Moscow, but also in St. Petersburg or in Karelia, in the Baltic States or the Urals. I recorded hours and hours of stories, sometimes interrupted by my interviewee's tears, sometimes by mine.

Some people revealed their names to me. Many did not want to go further than their first name and their patronymic name, and others in the end preferred to remain anonymous, refusing even to meet me. And as many people as wanted to tell their kommunalka experience, I was also able to determine how many were held back by modesty, by fear, and sometimes even by shame.

On the other hand, all man is a product of his era and I sadly noted with what ease the inhabitants of these apartments betrayed, without leaving out a single detail that could be useful for identification, all tied up neatly in a package, an old "neighbor" who they were "sure" had denounced their father or an acquaintance. In these cases it was I who preferred to draw the veil of anonymity over the informer. Even if the denunciation was obvious from the start as we see from the appendices that carry Lenin's hallmark, Vladimir Ilyich himself, who was the brains behind the kommunalka, who charged the People's Commissariat of Internal Affairs, the sinister NKVD, precursor of the Cheka and of the KGB, to find paid informers among the inhabitants of each apartment.

So kommunalka is a reflection of Soviet ideology in the daily life and in the personal experiences, conscious or unconscious, of tens of millions of Soviets? Not only. The heirs of the Soviets, that is the Russians, Ukrainians, Georgians, Armenians, Uzbeks, and so on today all still carry in their subconscious the vestiges of that period, as the director Andron Konchalovsky stressed in a recent book of meditations.

Reread Bulgakov, Pasternak, Solzhenitsyn, Alexei Tolstoy, after having read kommunalka, listen to the stories of old dissidents, look at contemporary Russian paintings, go see the film of the afore-mentioned Konchalovsky, of his brother Nikita Mikhalkov or of Pavel Lungin, see the plays of Ludmila Petrushevskaia, listen to the songs of Bulat Okudzhava and of Vladimir Vysotsky: the kommunalka is there, in today's Russia as in the former USSR.

I regretfully left Moscow in 2005, a city where I'd spent 15 years of my life and that I adore. I go there as often as I can, and notably I came back in 2008 to kommunalki: despite the disbelief of my friends and young people who think that the phenomena is part of a chapter of exotic memories now being capitalized on at auctions, I found them, right in the city center, in buildings where apartments renovated in "the European style," sell for between $2 and $10 million. The stories of people who still live with five or six families in five-room apartments shed light on a distinctive day in the "New Russia."

Moscow 1995, New York 2008–2010

NB: Out of 30 interviews, 28 were done between 1992 and 1995. The last interviews were dated April 2008.

CHAPTER 1

# "Uplotnienie": Filling Up

> She did not like the Gothic bed at all. It was too big. Even if Nicky in some miraculous way acquired a room six yards square, the medieval couch still would not fit into it.
> —Ilf & Petrov. *The Twelve Chairs*

My mother was a noblewoman.

She was descended from families close to the Tsar on my grandmother's side; and my grandfather was also a well-known aristocratic name. They lived in one of those select private hotels on the Arbat, but a short while before the Revolution, my mother, who was studying piano, decided to move closer to the Music Academy. She had just gotten married and rented an apartment on B...ski Street in a beautiful building belonging to a man called Ch...ov

The apartment was on the third floor: four large rooms in a row, a small one used as a closet that was near the bathroom, a 215-square-foot kitchen, a toilet, and then a bedroom. It was one of the few apartments in Moscow endowed with a bathroom. The windows looked out onto a garden that my mother had only to cross to reach the academy.

In 1914, as newlyweds, my father and mother moved into this building frequented by famous people such as Prince Yusupov[1] and other illustrious names of the old regime. Mother told me that all these men wore fur coats; these visions of elegantly attired famous men fascinated me, I who my entire life have only seen a completely different sort of man.

The "filling up" started five or six years after they had settled in this apartment with their dog, a mastiff adored by my father.

"Filling up," "Uplotnienie" in Russian, that's the extraordinary term that the Communists used to define the massive operation that consisted of installing into an apartment as many families as there were rooms, regardless of their origin or profession or personal history, all in the name of social equality and lack of space. For the leaders and primarily for Lenin, it was both a solution to the housing crisis and an ideological breakthrough. "So gentlemen, how do you explain these luxurious apartments? It is shameful. You must share them with the workers," the Bolsheviks said.

When I was born in 1927, the apartment had already been a "kommunalka" for six or seven years. Soviet society was in the midst of being restructured, and the ZHEK, or Bureau of Housing, which had offices in every building, ran the apartments with an authoritative hand. According to the new laws that were in effect, my parents had the right only to about 150 square feet, and they and the dog were confined to the main room, a pretty room with molding on the ceiling. The doors leading to the other rooms had been blocked up; we already had "the hallway system" in place, one of the nicknames for a way of life where families that are squeezed into a single room share the same hallway, the same kitchen, the same toilet and when there was one, the same bathroom.

The other rooms were occupied by three other families. There were ten of us in total, which sounds like a lot but is far from being a record. Each family had brought its own furniture, some of it old and worm-eaten, full of termites. They gnawed at my father's paintings, especially Aivazovsky's[2] seascapes, which my mother loved so dearly. My father was Polish, also of noble origin I think.

He was compelled to send the dog to the country, because three people living with a dog in a single room was simply impossible. The other tenants refused to allow the mastiff to sleep in the hallway; they already had trouble accepting my mother's fur coat hanging on a hook in the hall.

One day, months after having given the dog away, my father and I went by train to visit him in the suburbs. On leaving, we got in the last car of the train to watch him, the dog running alongside the tracks, tears streaming down my father's face. It was 1935, and I was seven. I still cannot think of this scene without crying.

Life in this apartment was even more difficult for my parents since we belonged to the old aristocratic class. "Here comes the Princess," the women would titter when mother entered the kitchen to prepare dinner. All the pretty curtains she had hung on the kitchen windows had been angrily torn down. On the mahogany cupboard left standing in the hallway, someone had carved with a nail "Oh my, what aristocrats!"

One of the families lived in the small room close to the bathroom. The man was kind, a Jewish intellectual who loved only his books. After he died, during the war, his wife sold all his books, and his daughter became a prostitute in order to survive. With mother—my father had already been taken away and shot by the People's Ministry for Internal Affairs, the NKVD,[3] by then—we would shut ourselves in our room in order not to hear, to forget.

This prostitute, barely older than I, was visited day and night by well-known people, politicians, and famous journalists. We heard this coming-and-going incessantly in the hallway as their room was at the very end, near the bathroom. As her daughter grew richer, the mother became stingier, until the day when worried about the electricity usage, she forbade the residents to use the hall light. As soon as we would step out of our bedrooms, we were plunged into total darkness.

Communal life is terrifying. The residents started to measure every square inch of the hallway and other common areas and to complain about the furniture—good furniture—that my mother had left here and there. They claimed that it took up too much space, that it had to be in our room, and that the hall didn't belong to us.

The "neighbors"[4] also measured the time we spent in the bathroom. In some communal apartments, the residents installed separate meters and light switches in the toilets so that each person used only their allotted electricity.

Despite all these petty actions, my mother could never bring herself to put the silverware in what she still considered to be her bedroom. She left all her cutlery in a sideboard in the kitchen and little by little saw all of her silverware disappear, stolen and shamelessly sold to the nearest pawnshop. One day, in one of these neighborhood shops, she spotted one of our housemates selling a piece of her silverware. She pretended not to see him.

I was always asking her: "Why do you leave all your nice dishes in the kitchen?" She would answer that it was a habit she could not break.

Today, I have only two spoons from that dinner service, which I jealously hold onto.

## 10 / Soviet Communal Living

This is how I grew up, terrified of my ancestry and enduring daily humiliation.

In order to live, my mother gave piano lessons to the sons of generals—the same generals who looted Germany of so many valuable paintings—who paid her with matches or hunks of bread.

I finished the Music Academy in 1952, always remaining in this apartment that I've lived in for some 30 years. At "home," I played the piano six hours a day, the "neighbors" constantly banging on our bedroom wall because we disturbed them.

CHAPTER 2

# White Army, Red Army

> Margarita Nikolaievna never touched a primus stove. Margarita Nikolaievna was ignorant of the horrors of life in a communal apartment.
>
> —Mikhail Bulgakov. *The Master and Margarita*

My father was a Bolshevik partisan; he didn't want to keep his father's surname—a tsarist colonel and White Army soldier. He was the illegitimate child of this colonel, an aristocrat, and his governess. After his wife's death, Colonel Lutin married my grandmother and gave my father a first-class education. However, everything unraveled during the Revolution. My father turned against his own father and half-brother; he even fought against them. Afterward, they both emigrated while my grandmother fled to Moscow with Father.

There she rented this huge apartment on Bolshaia Ordynka, which at the turn of the century was one of the prettiest streets in the center of town. I was born there, me, Liubov Vasilievna Zakharova—my father's new name—in 1918.

The ex-owner of the building had settled in a little house in the courtyard. In 1921, he had to give up the building to "Printing Shop No. 1," which was ensconced in this neighborhood. It was then that apartments started getting "filled." Ours did not escape.

I remember it, even though I was small, because my father had just come back from the Front. Due to the "filling up," of the entire apartment, my grandmother kept only an 86-square-foot room while my mother kept this large 182-square-foot room. My grandmother grew introverted. I don't know exactly how she felt about everything that had happened to us but I think she suffered greatly...It must be said, there were 35 of us living in the apartment!

Everybody worked in the printing house. Let's see...how many were there of us? "Tiotia Olia, Diadia Vasia, Igor, Liovka, Tiotia Zhenia, Vera Vasilievna, six, then in the other room eight: that makes fourteen, then Tiotia Tania and, what was her name again? Oh yes, Tiotia Polina..., nine in this other room, that makes twenty-three, then the Shcherbakovs, one, two, three, there were nine at the Shcherbakovs as well. Well, there were roughly 32 of us."

But they were good people. Vasily Ilyich Anisimov was a proofreader, Alexei Nikolaevich Shcherbakov was editor-in-chief. Komarov was an Old Believer; he stayed locked up in his room, didn't speak to anyone.

Some rooms were shared by two families, and not for a couple of days you know, but for years. Can you imagine two entire families in a single bedroom?

My father was, of course, a responsible civil servant, a member of the Party. That is why we were one of the privileged few. We had two rooms, three before my grandmother died. We even had a maid, Marusia. She slept in the room near the kitchen and used the toilets on the landing...No, no, she did not use the same toilets as the other 32 inhabitants....

Living in individual apartments was not the fashion. Even the director of the printing shop lived in a kommunalka.

Life was not hard then, strangely. It is much harsher now that there is only seven of us left here. My mother was a doctor. She would put on her coat at night and go cure the children of all the neighboring communal apartments.

When there were parties, all the women would make cakes, we would put the "patefon"[1] in the kitchen, bring out the vodka, and everybody danced.

Meanwhile, my father had become the head of the complex; he was somebody. We all treated each other with respect, using names and patronymics when addressing one another, not Tanka or Kolia like today.

At the beginning of the war, Lenochka Komarov was arrested in the middle of the night because she was against Stalin. It appeared that a colleague from work had denounced her. I was in Germany at the time, then in Poland. I was married and followed my husband who was a general, a squadron leader.

It was the good life but that did not last long. During the war, I was in the Krasnodar area. In 1945, I went to find my husband in Erevan, and there I found out that he had three wives!!!

So I returned to Moscow, and reinstalled myself in this apartment. Lenochka was still in prison. She came back in 1946. There were fewer of us but there were still a lot. Volodia Shcherbakov, one of the tenants, was a member of Stalin's guard corps. He told us stories about his work, especially about the days and nights spent guarding Stalin while he was vacationing at the Black Sea. Shcherbakov died young from lung cancer.

CHAPTER 3

# The Visit to Lenin

> ...wouldn't retribution be exacted, comrade Chekists, for that apartment, that woman, that smoky cat ? Would'nt someone ensconce in that living room some metalworker's lice-ridden family, who would use the grand piano for a toilet and force her to clean it out every morning, with her pink hands?
>
> —Nina Berberova, *The Accompanist*

My father was Jewish, my mother was Polish. They had received authorization to reside in St. Petersburg[1] thanks to my father's reputation, a well-known lawyer.

Born in 1902, I studied at the "Leteinaia" school whose benefactor was the Tsar's mother, Maria Federovna. The school did not accept Jews but my father knew how to handle himself and had succeeded in getting me enrolled. My tutor, Irène, was one of those Frenchwomen who had left her own country to come to Russia and educate the children of aristocratic and wealthy people.

Father collected art and assiduously frequented art dealers, often coming home with a painting. We had paintings signed by Rembrandt, Goya, Repin,[2] Levitan.[3] My father was very rich and at the time those paintings cost "groshi."[4]

We lived in a superb apartment on Nevski Prospect, six rooms on the third floor. After the Revolution, just before the flat became communal, some sailors came knocking on our door. "Orders from the top!" they said

**16 / Soviet Communal Living**

showing us a paper with a seal and stamp on it. They ransacked the apartment, taking canvases down, opening all the drawers and taking away, along with the paintings, all of Mother's jewelry.

My father could not endure my mother's tears. "Come," he told me, "we're going to Smolny."[5] I was 15 and so I traveled with father to Smolny to visit Vladimir Bonch-Bruevich, one of Lenin's pals.

We entered Smolny without a problem—my father could get in anywhere. While roaming the hallways in search of Bonch-Bruevich, we met Lenin.

"Who are you looking for?" he asked us. Father answered, "Bonch-Bruevich." "Come, I will show you the way," Lenin said to us.

Once in Bonch-Bruevich's office, Lenin said, "Sit down, talk to me." My father told about the sailors' visit and my mother's despair, and Bonch-Bruevich asked, "Could you recognize these three sailors?" "Yes, I remember them," I answered.

Then Vladimir Ilyich commanded Bonch-Bruevich: "Give them a car and two of our men so that they can search all of the houses where sailors are registered and get their belongings back."

The car immediately took us to an address where we found our three sailors and my mother's jewelry. The man who accompanied us ordered them to give back their loot, which they did.

The paintings, they too were recovered but a little later, not thanks to Lenin, but in a manner that said a lot about the way things worked at the time. A friend, who knew very highly placed people, phoned me and asked, "What is wrong E.? You look sad."

"It is not me," I answered. "It is Father who cannot reconcile himself to the loss of his Rembrandts and his Repin that the sailors took from him."

So a man, a Latvian, came to the house and telephoned someone in my presence, I don't know who and said, "You took paintings that belong to I. Bring them back. Immediately." That same day, my father had his paintings. They were confiscated for good some years later, to be exhibited in a museum.

After this luxurious and pampered childhood I wasn't unhappy despite spending practically all the rest of my life in the kommunalki of Leningrad and Moscow. Doubtless this is due to men, who loved me so much. My husband, an art critic, spoiled me all his life, and all of my suitors made me forget reality. At the theater, Mikhail Bulgakov once told me: "I do not know whether I liked the play, I did not watch it E., I was admiring you." My whole life has been measured by the poets or adventurers who wooed me. Some of these men, who I met in Vienna or Berlin, would have done anything to have me leave Soviet Russia—they told me the country was not for child-women like me.

But I love this country and no other. In Vienna, the owner of a luxurious hotel had fallen in love with me. "I beg you, please stay," he said to me. "I will put the hotel in your name. I will do everything for you."

"Not for anything on earth, my dear, I won't stay for anything on earth," I answered.

Once again I left and I have never regretted it.

CHAPTER 4

# Like Life in Naples

> Wasn't it this she was trying to escape to from her dingy communal apartment?
>
> —Anatoly Rybakov. *Children of the Arbat*

It was a luxury building on Chekhov Street, near Pushkin Square, in the very heart of Moscow. The building had been erected in 1916. Moscow, Kiev, and St. Petersburg had seen these splendid buildings spring up like mushrooms at the turn of the century. They were mostly owned by industrialists or important merchants of the First Guild.

My husband and I arrived in 1919, as "filling up" measures were all the rage. The owner had been evicted, and he had emigrated the day after the buildings' expropriation decree. His name was Bakulin, and some of the rooms of his first floor apartment were entirely covered with ivory. He also had a terrace adorned with plants that decayed very quickly and ended up becoming a sort of warehouse for the family occupying the living room.

We were housed on the sixth floor in an apartment of six rooms all in a row with a bathroom and an immense kitchen heated by a huge ceramic stove. For us, low-level bureaucrats, this place was an unheard of luxury; there was even an elevator. It seemed like a palace to us, 2,690 square feet with 14-foot-high ceilings... The building looked out onto the Hermitage Museum, we could hear music coming from the gardens.

**20** / Soviet Communal Living

But we were not alone...A couple without children lived in the first room, an employee of the *Izvestia*[1] and *Pravda*[2] printing houses. In the second one, there was a family "without rights," ex-homeowners deprived of their civil rights.[3] The man was the son of a textile industrialist, the woman also came from the wealthy bourgeoisie. They had been evicted from their select private hotel on Moskova and had made an attempt to recreate their world in a spacious 344-square-foot room. The authorities had not been too harsh with them and had allowed them to move in with their furniture, made of rare wood that they'd stacked up in the room making one corner a living room, one corner a dining area, and one corner a sleeping area...

In the next room lived a military family, the father had initially been a Tsarist cavalry officer before changing allegiance and joining the Red Army. He had a wife who was a bureaucrat, a daughter and a mother-in-law of unbelievable proportions, widow of a second rank officer.

We were given the fourth room with our young daughter. Next door to us lived a very sad railroad employee, Nikolai Petrovich, who had tuberculosis. His wife Masha had incredible energy. She washed laundry in order to raise their four children. The to-and-fro of clients bringing her their laundry never stopped during the day. From morning to night she frantically scrubbed shirts and sheets in the bathroom, our communal bathroom becoming completely inaccessible. She was constantly screaming and nothing was done without her approval.

In the room near the kitchen lived Niusha, an alcoholic who had been abandoned at birth. She had grown up in an orphanage before moving into our apartment. She gave birth to a little girl in the 1920s that she in turn abandoned, and that we never met.

Thus there were 18 of us in this apartment, sharing the same toilets, the same bathroom, and the same kitchen. The doors of our rooms were always open, everybody chatted to everybody, in the kitchen differences in provisions were not yet very noticeable, and everyone ate more or less the same food, essentially cabbage soup and kasha (boiled buckwheat).

During the war, the radio was always on, for New Year's we danced in the hallway. Potato sacks distributed at workplaces were stacked in the large hallway, from which emanated a strong smell of wet dirt throughout the entire apartment.

Despite the screams and dramas of this one and that one, it was very merry and congenial. It is where my daughter grew up. Dunia and the alcoholic Niusha mercilessly sized up her suitors while preparing their evening meal.

Laundry hung drying everywhere...just think about it...so many residents, each family with its own laundry line, in the bathroom, in the kitchen, or on the balcony. It was like life in Naples, in a way.[4]

CHAPTER 5

# I, Princess Golitsyn

> For the first few weeks in Moscow she camped anywhere she could. Then she was allotted a room in a communal apartment.
>
> —Alexey Tolstoy. *The Viper*

I was born 80 years ago on Bolshaia Molchanovka where we rented a vast apartment with three large rooms and two smaller ones. After finishing University, my father first settled in the country, on a large estate about 250 miles from Moscow, a little further out than Count Tolstoy's property. He then returned to live in the capital.

When the "filling up" decree was issued, at first we were of course invaded by hordes of neighbors, but then we were driven out from this place and that for years on end. My brother Ilarion Golitsyn, who keeps all the family archives, maintains that we were evicted from ten different places after the Revolution.

Many among the Golitsyn princes emigrated. We stayed because my father supported the first revolutionaries, the Mensheviks. He wasn't tsarist, and he thought that all his lands and numerous servants belonged to the past, to a bygone era. He very soon regretted not having chosen to emigrate.

My grandfather Vladimir Mikhailovich Golitsyn had been governor of Moscow. This portrait of him on the wall was painted by Valentin Serov.[1] The furniture that I have left, whatever I was able to move into ever-smaller rooms is partly from the Golitsyn princes, partly from my mother's family, the Bobrinsky princes. The table here looks anachronistic; it was probably built by serfs. It is made of very heavy oak—with its leaves open, it is wider than this room.

I have lived in communal apartments nearly all my life. I never spoke of my noble origins and my husband who was of lesser nobility, didn't speak of his origins either. The other inhabitants were from a modest background: a singer and her mother, a concierge and his family. We had a kitchen with a kerosene stove. There weren't any major quarrels; mainly clashes over the divvying up of electrical bills and cleaning up the common living areas, but my silver spoons all disappeared one by one.

We did not have hot water or a washroom. After the war there were up to 24 inhabitants. Among the newcomers was a prince, Vladimir Nikolaevich Dolgorukov. We both knew who the other was but we didn't say anything. He had very aristocratic manners and immense piety, like many Russian noblemen. Very sweet, he never raised his voice and was kind to everyone.

My husband went away to the front and never came back. His last letter is dated November 1941, posted near Volokolamsk.[2] I never found out how he died; I do not know where he is buried.

My elder sister emigrated to France after her husband's death. She lives in Clamart.[3] I went to visit her a few years ago.

Our relatives abroad started coming back to Moscow around 1963–64, the Khrushchev years. None of them came to our place; they were afraid and we were too. So in actual fact they never truly understood what our communal apartments were really like.

Of course, when I look at this portrait of my grandmother, her crinolines and marvelous hats, I tell myself it must be pleasant to live in one's own house, to have one's own garden and especially, to have servants. But we tried to survive with our dignity intact; what was going to happen was going to happen. I worked a lot—day and night—and I tried not to pay attention to the meanness of daily life: the neighbor who turns you in because you had a relative sleeping in your room or the doorman sneakily interrogating you about your past.

But in our kommunalka, I was the only one who never made a cake to celebrate the October Revolution.

CHAPTER 6

# Spy Stories

> When Olga in her thin cotton dressing-gown, with her hair disarranged and her face gloomy, appeared in the kitchen, everyone stopped talking—only the primus stoves, full of paraffin and suppressed fury—continues hissing away.
>
> —Alexey Tolstoy. *The Viper*

**1st spy story**: Richard Sorge[1] and my sister Ekaterina Alexandrovna Maximova lived together in a communal apartment in a semi-basement, at No. 11 Kislovsky, a cul-de-sac near the Arbat. After returning from Italy where her husband had died of tuberculosis, Katia first stayed there with a friend who was registered in the apartment.

When entering from the street, you had to go down a grimy staircase before being enveloped by a filthy, dimly lit corridor. At the end of the corridor was a communal kitchen where almost a dozen petroleum stoves burned simultaneously.

It was an eight-room apartment without a bathroom. Eight families lived there. My sister slept in her friend, Dora Isakovna's, room.

After her son, accused of being Trotskyite, was arrested, Dora Isakovna lost her mind and was committed to a mental institution. Katia was left alone. It was at that time that she began giving Russian lessons to Willy Stahl[2] in the small room in her kommunalka. One day Stahl arrived with a friend and told her: "This man would also like you to give him Russian lessons, Katia." It was Richard Sorge.

This was 1928 or 29, she was 24 or 25 then and had a lot of charm; men always noticed her.

During one of her stays in Petrozavodsk in Karelia[3] where we were living then, she told us she had met an extraordinary man, a German researcher. "If I never saw him again, I would still never forget him," she said. He wrote her from Germany to tell her that he was sending her a package. In fact it was a suitcase full of clothing and shoes.

He would send her little parcels, often slipping in a little something, which gave a clue as to his whereabouts, like a tiny bit of soap with Paris written on it, a photo of New York' s harbor, a little postcard.

At first Katia was unaware that Richard was a secret agent. She knew he worked for Comintern,[4] and that he carried out investigations. When he left for Japan, shortly after their wedding, she knew about his work but not all the details.

The inhabitants of the flat were numerous and nice, but Katia had very little contact with them since she had no interest in cooking; she and Sorge often ate in restaurants.

But obviously, everybody had noticed him even before he'd settled in. He had a different sort of look about him, wearing a long leather coat, and he didn't look like a Soviet. When Richard returned from China without warning Katia of his impending arrival, she was at work. As she arrived home in the evening, she found all the doors in the corridor ajar and the apartment gossips informed her that "the stranger" had been around asking for her...

She would always use his bathroom when he stayed in a hotel room; she couldn't wash at her own place. He would prepare a hot bath when she arrived at the end of the day. She told me how much he enjoyed holding out her robe for her...

They decided to live together and settled in this damp basement. He did not stay in it for a long time.

I remember that apartment. Katia's room was the next to last at the end of the corridor. The window was tall and looked out on the sidewalk. All you saw were the legs of the passer-bys.

The furniture in the room consisted of Dora Isakovna's bed, a huge trunk on which Katia slept, and a little sofa. I would often sleep on the floor. After Dora Isakovna was committed, Katia could finally sleep in a real bed.

An incredible mess reigned in the room. Books were piled in every corner. The corridor was filthy, and the kitchen stank of petroleum. The walls were black with soot and cockroaches.

The worst was that there wasn't even any water in the kitchen. Everybody used the one and only sink in the hallway; to wash themselves, to cook, and to clean their pots and pans. Eight families sharing this one source of water...

Katia's room was heated with a small radiator. They were married just before his departure to Japan. He never came back.

Katia brought me Sorge's leather coat with its removable fur lining when she came to Karelia, because she was afraid it would get stolen. It was extremely easy to get into their room and some of Richard's stuff, a very valuable camera for example, had already disappeared. I kept the coat for many years before finally donating it to the Museum of the City of Leningrad in 1965, along with other souvenirs of Richard's travels like a wooden ashtray, a Chinese alarm clock, and a German watch.

In this little room, they conceived a child who was never born. She had sent him a letter as soon as she found out she was pregnant. He had responded enthusiastically. He told her that he had started buying children's clothes and that if it was a girl they'd call it Katia after her. Rim, an Estonian man working for the Secret Service in the cipher department told me how surprised they had been to suddenly hear him talk of children's clothing.

Letters didn't get sent by normal mail, of course. Somebody would bring them to her. A general, Mikhail Ivanovich Ivanov, often came to see her in this damp basement and brought her parcels or letters. She would ask, "General, couldn't they send someone else instead of him?" He'd answer that he was a very hard man to replace.

One day, when I was visiting my sister, a woman came to see her. Once in the room, the woman, a stranger to my sister, said in a low voice: "How are you? He is very worried about your health." Katia refused to answer and said, "I will write to him myself." The woman had brought a letter from Sorge. The Secret Service had probably sent her instead of General Ivanov because of the pregnancy.

Katia then wrote him the news that there would not be a child. It upset him deeply.

When leaving for Japan, he had asked his superiors for Katia to finally get better lodging since they were now married. Orders were given and she soon moved into an individual apartment in a guarded, heavily watched building. However, she was alone from then on.

28 / Soviet Communal Living

She was born on December 4, 1904. She was 39 when she died. Sorge was 10 years older when the Japanese executed him. I discovered the whole story about the spy Richard Sorge much later in the '60s when the Soviet authorities turned him into a real cult hero.

**2nd spy story**: I knew my husband Leon Borovich was a spy but I only found out long after his death that he and Richard Sorge had worked together. He was shot in 1937 on Stalin's orders.

Before leaving for China in 1936, we lived in a communal flat in a four-story building in the center of Moscow. Four families shared it. All were agents' families, linked to Comintern in one way or another, but no one knew precisely what the others' activities were.

There were Jews, Russians, and Latvians. Everyone had a room; we had two, and in one of them was enthroned a Dutch stove.

One of the two Latvians was a midget living alone, and the second was a radio engineer working for the Ministry of Communication. He was married to Lucette D., a French girl who spoke Russian very well. She worked for the French sector of Radio-Moscow and was, without a doubt, a spy as well.

Lucette had a friend, Claire, who was also French and who often came to see them. Claire sported the Order of the Red Star[5] on the lapel of her jacket; she also spoke perfect Russian.

We left for China in April 1936. My daughter Svetlana was born there in Shanghai. We came back in July 1937. They arrested my husband a few days after our return and shot him. I found everything out 27 years later, in 1964, when the Sorge affair was revealed in the press.

Life became much harder with the war. I was an engineer and worked in a factory. Moscow started getting bombed. The Latvian left for the army, and Lucette for France. She left the Soviet Union in 1940. She received permission to visit her father Pierre. I never saw her again.

Her husband left us her piano to take care of. "It will get out of tune with the humidity. Your room is better heated."

But soon we were unable to have heat anymore and then rats appeared. From 1941 to 1942, we found refuge with Svetlana in Tashkent, in Central Asia. I came back to Moscow in 1942, but the atmosphere in the apartment was different.

One of the inhabitants was Hungarian. Relations between the USSR and Hungary had deteriorated and expulsion orders were raining down.[6]

The authorities gave her 24 hours to leave Soviet territory. She was roughly 50 years old. She committed suicide, probably on the same day she received her expulsion notice.

The police kept coming for a few days. They would ask us, "Do you know where your neighbor is?" but we had not seen her and the door of her room was closed. In a kommunalka one does not go into a neighbor's room without being invited. Co-tenants can sometimes spend a lifetime without seeing all the rooms in the apartment.

After a week of fruitless visits, they finally decided to tear down the door. They found her hanging by a belt from the chandelier. We had been living with a corpse in the apartment for a week without knowing it.

I didn't have the strength to sign the official report.

CHAPTER 7

# The Black Crow

> In 1919, they took away three of the professor's five rooms. Then he declared to Maria Stepanovna: If they don't put an end to this nonsense, Maria Stepanovna, I will leave the country.
> —Mikhail Bulgakov. *The Fatal Eggs*

I do not know who denounced him. Our co-tenants, the inhabitants of the building, his clients—he was a legal counselor—someone else altogether? It did not matter in any case. Moscow was jam-packed with informants, and even if he had hidden all of his documents and burnt all traces of his past, my father was expecting it.

It was in 1937, I was 10 years old. My father taught me poetry, he was a refined man who loved receiving people and prepared wonderful celebratory dinners.

Our table had everything: crab salad, black caviar, he also bought little light biscuits with which he made a cake by adding butter, coffee, and cognac. Everyone at the house was jealous, even though the women made fun of him in the kitchen.

That evening, Dad tucked me in tightly, as he did every night, on the small couch in our room where I slept close to them. The bell rang in the middle of the night, three times, which meant it was for us. Some kommunalki have the same number of doorbells as tenants, with little nameplates for each one, and the bell rings in the appropriate room. At our house it was only the number of rings that determined who was being visited.

They weren't happy with simply ringing the bell, they started banging their fists on the door. The horror of that noise will stay with me forever. The hullabaloo got everyone out of bed but nobody came out of their room. They had all guessed what was happening.

They came into our room. I saw a soldier in uniform, accompanied by a plumber who worked in the building—the infamous "witness" who had to participate in arrests. My father, he knew that they had come to take him away.

It was "Chernyi Voron," the black crow,[1] the van was parked in the street. Many Russians of my generation or even younger still wake up with a start when a car engine disturbs the silence of the night and stops in front of their house.

The men from the NKVD searched the room but found nothing other than my mother's musical scores and my father's books. All the documents proving that my father had served in the Tsarist army for a few months had been destroyed.

Then, Father gently took off the ring he wore on his finger, a black sapphire inherited from his mother, and slid it on Mother's finger. He was barely 40. We never saw him again, never had any news of him, never knew where he was. He was Polish, of noble origin and had a law degree from Moscow University.

Our "neighbors" did not know his surname, but he addressed his wife with a polite Polish expression: "proshu pani" (please). One didn't need to be a psychic to "unmask" him.

The co-tenants had probably heard everything through the walls. The next day, in the kitchen, they pretended that nothing had happened. During the rest of the 15 years I spent in this communal apartment, in the frightening lack of privacy living with three other families, no one ever mentioned a word about my father, who disappeared forever one night in 1937.

A year after his arrest, as Mother was exhausting herself running in vain from one prison to another, a man paid us a visit. He reeked of vodka even though he'd sprayed himself liberally with cologne to hide the smell. He told us that he had been detained in the same cell as my father, that my father cried like a child unceasingly, and that he had asked him to bring me a balloon.

I loved balloons when I was little; what's more, I still love them.

CHAPTER 8

# Even the Baltics

> The apartment in which Michel was living was a communal one. It had ten rooms and thirty-odd occupants. Michel had nothing to do with these people and even shunned them and avoided becoming acquainted with anyone.
>
> —Mikhail Zoshchenko. "Michel Sinyagin"
> *(Nervous People and Other Satires)*

My mother was French. Her name was Marie Augustine Dupont, and she was born in Collonges-sous-Salève, near the Swiss border. She had studied in Geneva where she'd met my father whose name was Blumfeld, and who was Estonian of German origin. I was named Nancy when I came into this world on October 26, 1906, in St. Petersburg. Like my mother's best friend, Nancy Renard.

Dad was the director of a factory. I had the typical childhood of well-to-do St. Petersburg families. A Russian "niania" (nanny) and a German governess. We spoke French at home even with my father, but I spoke Russian with my brothers, because of school.

We fled from St. Petersburg during the Revolution. The communists were after my father. We went to join his sister who lived in Estonia. I remember that horrendous journey, it was 11 already. It lasted several days. We had to go from one station to another, we didn't even have tickets; trains were bursting with fleeing refugees.

We arrived in Estonia, a Baltic country then occupied by Germans. I did my studies in German in the city of Pärnu[1] where we first settled.

My father's business continued to prosper. Estonia and the other Baltic countries became independent after World War I—they were only annexed by the USSR in 1940, and I was a very free young girl. That is how at the age of 18, I spent a year in Austria staying at an aunt's place.

When I came back my parents had moved to Tallinn, the Estonian capital; they knew everybody, they were socialites.

I left again, this time for London where I studied at Pitman's College. It was Mr. Dehaye, my father's Belgian associate, who insisted that I learn business correspondence. It bored me to death. I lived at their house. I remember the typing courses, the girls ready, hands held high over the keyboard, and at the signal they would start typing extremely fast. I looked at them in a stupor, I found it so stupid. Other than the typing, I enjoyed life in London, I felt at home. I had met the little Dehayes in kindergarten in St. Petersburg, Peggy Dehaye was my friend. Their mother was English but in London among themselves the Dehayes spoke Russian, a horrendous Russian.

My mother also spoke Russian very badly. Her friends, all the Russian nobility of St. Petersburg, almost everyone spoke French with her, it was more chic.

After staying in London, I spent a few months in Rome. I went through museums, I walked around. I was an au pair on Corso Vittorio Emanuele, an elegant street in the center. I was about 20, I wasn't really studying. I led the itinerant life of a young, free, and rich girl. I also lived in a convent that took in young girls of good family—it was at that time that I saw the Pope. I remember the crowd screaming "Viva il Papa" on St. Peter's Square and how it was like waves of sound.

My European tour having come to an end, I returned to Estonia where I married a brilliant Estonian officer called Vaharo. We had a little daughter Angela and a few years of happiness; during this period, we lovingly had a house built for us in Nomne, a suburb of Tallinn, here where we are meeting today. The architect, a friend of my husband's, was famous. I drew the plans for the interior and took care of the decorating. We had very nice furniture, old master paintings...

But then "THEY" arrived. The Soviets invaded Estonia. They riddled our little country with military bases. They arrested the three of us and took us to Peskula, to a camp. There they separated us. Husbands on one side, wives and children on the other. The camp was full. They also brought people from Latvia there.

I never saw my husband again. Angela and I were exiled to the Kirov area, near Siberia. I never knew exactly what my status was. My only document was a little bit of paper on which was written that I was an "officially displaced person." I worked in a sovkhoz, a state farm. At first it was amusing enough because they brought us by bus to this farm every morning and left us there to do what we wanted. I am no country girl, I don't know much about this stuff but I found it interesting at first.

I lived with some peasants with another exiled Estonian, a commandant's wife who also had a child.

I was unaware that my husband had been executed. I did not fully understand the horror of the situation.

I spent 16 years in that place. The director of the sovkhoz had chosen me because she knew I was rich and came from Estonia, which meant I had goods to bargain with. All these little deals were obviously done secretly in exchange for small favors. There were bedbugs all over the walls where I lived. A friend told me that was where she saw me cry for the first time, because of the bedbugs and the dirt.

In the fields I had to cut and tie sheaves of wheat. I recognized mine because they were so poorly done. The machines would break down often, and we would have nothing to do for hours, just like that, waiting.

After the first year, I started teaching thanks to a German woman, a communist. Her husband was detained in a concentration camp in Germany, and she had managed to escape to Leningrad from where she'd been sent to my area. We soon got to know each other, she was very kind. She offered me this job because I was the only one who knew German. That is how I taught, for a very long time, even if I was not supposed to officially.

We lived such a miserable life, everyone was so poor…Sometimes, while walking I would tell myself, "I have to wake up, I have to wake up." It was like a nightmare from which I had to wake up. But then life would go on: you had to get up, go to work, keep on going.

For many months, at first we thought that the Germans would kick the communists out that it couldn't last long.

When World War II ended, and I understood that the Germans would not drive out the communists, I organized my escape with Angela. I had an aunt, my Austrian aunt, who lived near Batumi[2] in Georgia,

**36** / Soviet Communal Living

her husband was in the militia. So we ran away with my daughter, we fled.

A teacher who lived with us had said that the kolkhoz[3] workers who were going to a place called Libiazhy could take us in their sleigh. It was 1945, we had successfully escaped—from Okunievo, where we lived, to Libiazhy, where there were boats, then from there to Katielnich to take the train.

I had no identification papers at all but nobody had any, not even the kolkhoz workers, otherwise they could have fled to the city to try and have a less horrible life, and that was something Stalin wanted to avoid at all costs!

We arrived at the boat just as the police were arresting a salesman from Tallinn who was also trying to flee. We were lucky, they did not find us, and we miraculously managed to get on an overcrowded train. My daughter was already in the train compartment and kept screaming: "Mother, Mother." Someone lifted me, and thanks to him, I found myself in the compartment.

We stayed in Batumi, on the Black Sea, for a year. I worked in a music school, teaching Italian to Georgian opera singers!

Obviously they found me, it took them months to find me, and they sent me back to the sovkhoz[4] in Siberia . . .

When I was there, in Okunievo, I had to go several times a year to register at a police station 15 kilometers away. I went on foot, whatever the weather, in winter as in summer; in winter, wolves would lie in wait.

I could see wolf tracks in the snow while walking. I am a Catholic like my mother, I prayed to the Virgin Mary to let me pass without the wolves finding me.

Children from surrounding kolkhozes also went on foot to the school where I taught German and Russian. One day a female wolf caught one of the children who was playing around the frozen pond. The wolf took him, and we only found his little coat. The wolf had eaten the child.

One day I got arrested by the police who accused me of having made anti-Stalin comments. Undoubtedly someone had denounced me. They took me to Kirov[5] where I was held in prison for two months. They were forced to admit in the end that I had done nothing. Thirty years later, I received a letter by mail informing me that the file detailing that interrogation had been destroyed!!!

In 1958, when I came back to Estonia after our rehabilitation, my house had become a communal apartment. My beautiful house that I had spent so much care and passion to plan and decorate, this house which was the culmination of my husband's and my love. It was before the nightmare, I had come back, my husband had disappeared, I had spent 18 years in the snow among the wolves, and I found my house was occupied.

In my bedroom lived two older people and in the living room and in my husband's study lived a family of three. A couple with two children, the Mullers, occupied another bedroom and an old spinster lived in my boudoir... Ten people in total, all Estonian.

At first we went to stay across the street because fortunately my mother had kept her house in the same neighborhood. To make the tenants leave was extremely complicated, it was mainly my daughter who took care of it. You surely know the stories of these deals, these trades worked out to reclaim rooms. It took us some time to get everybody out of there and to be able to settle in again. Everything inside was broken though. The furniture was damaged, many objects had disappeared.... First, German officers had inhabited the house, then the Soviets, before becoming a communal apartment.

Because we had been rehabilitated, they had to accept our solutions for a compromise and give us back our house.

But they could not give me back my husband.

CHAPTER 9

# The Siege of Leningrad

> You'll agree that to have a separate apartment of your own is after all a pretty bourgeois thing to do. People ought to live together, in a collective family, and not lock themselves up in some private fortress.
> —Mikhail Zoshchenko. "A Summer Breather"
> (*Nervous People and Other Satires*)

When the big bombing of Leningrad started, on the night of the 7th to the 8th of November 1941, I was living with my mother in a large apartment on Giliarovsky Prospect, today known as Chkalov.[1] Four families, all wealthy and taken care of by servants, shared these seven rooms when the war started. Despite the "filling up" and communal living, many ex-bourgeoisies had kept their servants after the Revolution.

Three of the four families had been "evacuated" out of Leningrad, and they had left their maids behind to keep an eye on the place and to make sure nothing disappeared from their rooms.

I was seven years old, and at first my mother had decided to have me leave the city. I was already in the train when she suddenly changed her mind. She rushed into the compartment, took me in her arms, and came out again, not even attempting to get my suitcase. She did well, the train got bombarded, and there were few survivors.

So then we went to live with my aunt to get through those horrendous times all together. At the beginning of the war, many Leningrad families

**40** / Soviet Communal Living

joined together to help each other, at least among parents. I say among parents because as to the rest...

In order to ring the apartment bell, you had to pull a little string. In our room there was my aunt, her old maid and the maid's daughter, my mother and I, and a student of my aunt's. My aunt's son was killed the night of December 31, 1941, and my grandmother who also lived there died of hunger during the winter. As for me, I was still going to kindergarten where I was fed a little. It was less difficult for me than for others.

I was never afraid, maybe out of stupidity but mainly because I was young, and also I was a little boy, and we all wanted to be heroes. I was convinced that the Germans would never take Leningrad. I even felt a sense of freedom, I walked around the city. I know a boy who went out for a walk and never came back.

This apartment was different because it was huge and practically empty, all the inhabitants had evacuated. We spent the first winter talking about food, telling each other what we had eaten before the war.

We were allowed 125 grams of bread per day, 150 for workers. Milk and flour disappeared completely until the spring of 1942.

The apartment had no water or electricity. We went to fetch rusty-smelling water near the Moscow train station and lit the rooms with a small tinplate bottle filled with kerosene in which a wick lay soaking.

My grandmother died of hunger; she had given her ration card to the maid's daughter. We wrapped her in a sheet and brought her to the collection area where all the corpses were brought. It was always so crowded. People who had died in communal apartments and who didn't have parents were brought in by neighbors, who usually took a few days to notice they'd died.

Each person lived in their room, keeping the door closed to retain the heat and prepared their pitiful daily meal: some tea or just hot water, some fat, and crumbs. When we found some additional food, obviously we ate it together, as a family. Solidarity within the apartment walls had its limits: we fetched water from the "little Neva"[2] together, or stood in line for bread, but that was about it.

When the Germans bombarded, we didn't go down into the shelter, we would hide behind the cupboards or under the beds. We all know dozens of people who did not survive the famine. Like the sister of the woman who would later become my wife, who died at the age of 10—it was March 25. On the 19th, their mother had given birth to a little boy in the same room where her eldest daughter lay dying.

In the apartment where I lived, two cleaning ladies died of hunger, even though they were young and healthy; we heard them moaning in their employer's room. They only had ration cards for unproductive citizens. In 1941 that meant certain death because they were allowed less than 100 grams of bread per day. Mother had managed to get the other tenants employed in the factory where she worked and that is how she saved them. They received workers' ration cards.

As for my mother, she became extremely thin and anemic. In 1942, she gave birth to a child who died at the hospital.

A woman of about 40 moved into the room of the servant who had died. She received many visitors, men who paid her in food. We had a polite relationship but sometimes it was very difficult for us; we were so hungry. She never gave anything to anyone. It was everyone for oneself.

Army personnel were among her "friends." In December 1941, when there was a total shortage and even bread had disappeared, somebody knocked at our door at three in the morning. It was her coming to tell us that they were selling bread in the street. We rushed down in the middle of the night to buy what we could. So she wasn't wicked, but in a famine nobody gave away whatever they could get in addition to their regular rations.

In another room, there were refugees whose house had been destroyed in a bombardment. A woman and her two children, aged three and five. She was so hungry that she even ate her children's food. We heard through the wall, the little boy, the eldest, asking her where there was certain food because he'd heard on the radio it could be found in the city. One of this woman's children died of hunger; I can't remember now which one of the two. She left the kommunalka after that.

We were all so weak. We broke the furniture to make a fire. But one day the neighbors stole the wood that my mother had gathered and piled up in the corridor. My childhood books were also burnt, along with anything flammable in the cupboards, including things from the rooms of the evacuees.

We knew that certain inhabitants were stealing but we couldn't do anything about it. We were too weak, and it wouldn't have done any good. Many valuable objects were stolen and sold on the black market. During the years of the blockade, silverware and paintings were exchanged for a glass of milk or a bit of bread.

## 42 / Soviet Communal Living

In 1944, when the evacuees started returning, there were lawsuits. Some found their rooms occupied by refugees who the authorities did not know where to relocate. Tensions rose between those who had stayed and those who were returning because we, we had lived through the blockade and its atrocities and we felt like victims, or heroes at least, while the evacuees accused us of allowing their rooms to be pillaged when they weren't whispering that we had stolen everything ourselves.

At the university where I teach geometry, there are many colleagues who survived the blockade, we still sometimes speak about it. For example, one of my colleagues lived with her family in an apartment where their room was heated due only to her father's ingenuity. There were seven of them in that room, two of whom were children and that winter the barometer went down to -40. In the morning when she'd wake up with her little sister, they'd be dressed warmly as if they were going outside, and then walked in the corridor and the adjoining room where it was freezing. For their mother it was a walk because they'd had some "fresh air." My colleague told me how one day she'd found some abandoned toys in one of the rooms and had taken them, and how afterward it felt as though she had been in a shop.

When the "road of life"[3] was opened, around March 1942, across Lake Ladoga, an electric cable was installed under the ice, feeding the factories but not the houses, no, not yet. As of spring 1942, the city slowly sprang to life again. Theaters and the zoo reopened.

In the USSR, communal apartments always have to have at least one drunk, it's part of the communal landscape. During the blockade, the drunks were the first to die because they were deprived of this highly caloric daily ration. Big smokers also died faster then others. They had less will to fight.

CHAPTER 10

# The Denunciation

"For thirty rubles," he said, "I can fix you up in a bathroom [...] You can live in the bathroom. It has no windows, of course, but it does have a door."
—Mikhail Zoshchenko. "The Crisis" (*Nervous People and Other Satires*)

Before the Revolution, the apartment near the Patriarch Pond[1] had belonged to a German pharmacist named K.

K. lived in those six rooms with his wife M. and their two daughters, N. and M. There was also a servant's room for the maid.

When the apartment became communal after the Revolution, they were left with only two rooms. In the other four, four families were installed, one of which was mine, the Z., a modest Jewish family. My mother, an accountant, had arrived from Ukraine at the beginning of the civil war; her family had fled the pogroms. My father was a Jew from Ukraine as well.

In 1935 when I was born, K. had already died and M. lived with her two daughters, one of whom, N., was handicapped. M. was very beautiful, tall, distinguished, and elegant. You could see she had known other society than Soviet society. Only M. was working; I think the three of them mainly survived by selling off family jewelry and their precious china bit by bit. I still have a plate that belonged to them.

44 / Soviet Communal Living

The mother was a fervent admirer of Ivan Sergeievich Kozlovsky, the opera singer. She and her daughters never missed a performance; the walls in their room were covered with his portraits. They knew him, and they had been to his place. In the apartment, people said that her passion for the theater was one of the causes of her daughter's disability: she had dropped her one evening when she was late. The "neighbors" always told all sorts of nonsense about the other inhabitants, especially about those who surround themselves with mystery.

In addition to us and the K.s, there was also a family of architects with two children, then a couple with their son, the G. and, very important to the rest of the story, another couple, of which the man, N.M. was a prosecutor. His wife called him "birdie," and she was his "kitten." It appears that "birdie" and "kitten" were at the origin of one, if not of many of the tragedies we had to live through in this apartment.

In 1936, G. was taken away by the NKVD, and he never came back. I don't know exactly who he was, what he did, or who had denounced him. His wife only found out several years later that he had died in the Gulag.[2]

At first the apartment was heated with wood, then with gas. In the kitchen, everyone had their own oil heater. Later they installed gas stoves for us. Every family had its own small table and storage space but everyone ate in their own room. You don't eat in the kitchen in a kommunalka, you only prepare food there, and it's a place where you chat, where you shout, and where you settle collective problems . . .

In 1941, G.'s son was on vacation in Ukraine, staying with some family. He was about 14. When the Germans occupied Ukraine, they sent him to work in Holland. He chose to stay there, and a few years later he became an architect and got married.

One day, some KGB men came to see Mrs. G., asking her to write to her son to get him to come back to the USSR—there too, who had alerted them? She didn't want to do it; she knew what it could mean. But they forced her. She wrote the required letter, but fortunately her son guessed and he never came back. He knew the Gulag awaited him on his return. He was considered a traitor to his country. Everyone who came back to the USSR right after the war had the same end. So this woman over a span of a few years, found herself a widow and then was separated from her teenage son, forced to keep him at a distance in order to save him.

I was old enough to understand at the time. And there was talk in the apartment, his mother and mine were friends, and I was all ears.

Sometimes there were arguments, when people live in such proximity, it's inevitable. One toilet, one single bathroom, and so many different people, all strangers to each other. But we didn't complain, and I have a wonderful memory of the special atmosphere that reigned in this house.

I had friends who lived in individual apartments; they always wanted to come to my place, our 15-square-meter room where we were numerous and on top of each other. They found it "interesting," our apartment was interesting.

When the war started, the authorities ordered the deportation of Germans from Moscow. M. was already sick at the time. In order for her not to be deported, the K.s tried to have her pass as a Jew. But someone denounced them, doubtless our prosecutor N.M. They received an order to leave Moscow. Meanwhile M. was already dying, I remember coming into her room, she handed me a cloth, asking me to clean Kozlovski's portrait. Terrified at the idea of being deported, her daughters left her for several days in the room after she had drawn her last breath.

Of course, we couldn't prove that it was the prosecutor who denounced them but what happened afterward does prove it. All the inhabitants of the apartment were afraid of him and had a very formal relationship with him, which is not very easy when you live together.

When N. and M. were obliged to say that their mother had died, they tried to hide their jewelry. They put gold in the doorknobs but the NKVD agents who came to search the apartment, had apparently been warned, they instantly went to remove the doorknobs.

I remember it being unbearable for me as a child to see these two young women, so polite, so distinguished, whom I adored, suddenly being treated like vulgar criminals, stripped of everything, and taken away. They were deported to the mines of Karaganda, in Kazakhstan. N. the invalid, who had weak lungs, died there, no doubt she couldn't take the coal dust.

M. came back a few years later, thanks to Kozlovsky's intervention. She was given a room in a kommunalka on the Arbat,³ where her life continued to be a nightmare. I do not know whether she is still alive.

In our place, K.s' two rooms were given to a KGB worker and his family. He was kind; he'd go hunting and bring back meat that he'd distribute to everybody. He did not hide his affiliation with the KGB, we

**46** / Soviet Communal Living

felt somewhat uneasy in his presence which feeling he tried in vain to dissipate.

He left quickly and a new happy period began in the kommunalka. The prosecutor also moved away shortly after the K.s got deported.

A family of musicians moved in. The woman had a music program on the radio. They organized parties in their room where a piano was enthroned and received singers from the Bolshoi.[4] I heard everything from my room, it was fascinating.

We did not have a television at the time, and the woman's stories were captivating. She always had a story to tell when we would all gather in the kitchen.

In the prosecutor's old room, lived a German-Russian interpreter and her son. She was delightful as well, her husband had died during the war, and she taught military translators at the academy.

There were twelve of us inhabitants. Around 5 p.m., the kitchen filled up with women, one at the stove, another one cut stuff, a third stayed seated, smoking a cigarette. Sometimes we ate seeds and chatted.

Everyone was interested in what happened to the others. We would compare boyfriends and shared cakes. The women compared their baking talents. Each night, after having dinner in our respective rooms, we would all reunite in the kitchen, everyone would sit where they could and the day's tales would start.

The radio journalist, for example, once was present during a visit of the Shah of Iran and of his wife Soraya and told us how the whole studio kept staring at Soraya until a beautiful Russian actress, Alla Larionova, entered and eclipsed all the women present, including the Shahbanu.[5] We listened like at the theater, religiously.

At the time, German prisoners were employed constructing buildings in Moscow. Because they were hungry, they would knock on doors and ask for bread. And we were astounded to see the interpreter, whose husband had been killed by these Germans, for whom we nursed an official hatred, give them food and talk to them. This woman, as well as others, taught me a lot. My life would probably have taken another turn, less intellectual, had I not lived in this communal apartment.

Near the kitchen there was an office that had become a storeroom. I would spend entire days foraging through the K.s' abandoned stuff, I read books and above all a pre-Revolutionary journal *Vokrug Sveta, Around the World.*

Everyone decorated their own room according to their taste, their background, and their means, of course. The K.s and the family of musicians had antique furniture and objects we did not know existed for a while. Our furniture was much more modest, probably without taste. These cultural gaps had a profound effect on me, coming from a simple family. I probably would not have gone so much to the opera had I not heard so much of it behind my room's wall.

The interpreter had a maid who slept in the corridor behind a curtain. Her name was Liuba, she came from the countryside.

Liuba progressively lost her mind. First, she started writing little love notes to the musician that she slipped under his door. His wife told us about it in the kitchen. We all thought it was a joke in the beginning, but the game went on for a while. Then Liuba started pacing in the corridor. She would walk up and down, all day long singing in a strange voice. The song itself was odd, and she swung her head. Some months later, the interpreter called a doctor who diagnosed her with a sort of insanity. She was committed.

CHAPTER 11

# Summer 1948

> Bormenthal raised his voice. Sharikov stepped back, took three slips of paper from his pocket –one green, one yellow, and one white—and, poking his finger at them, said:
> "Here. Member of the tenants' Association. Assigned an area of sixteen square arshin."
>
> —Mikhail Bulgakov. *Heart of a Dog*

My wife and I lived in a kommunalka in the Preobrazhensky distrcit in the northeast of Moscow. A two-story wooden house, without toilets, without a bathroom, no hot water of course, that we shared with two other families and my in-laws. I had just finished my medical studies and was already practicing as a surgeon.

We were spending our vacation on the Black Sea that summer, in a rest home in Gagra, in Abkhasia. One day, as we were walking along the coastal road, a black limousine passed us, then slowed down and stopped, giving us time to catch up with it. Before the car started off again, I had time to recognize Lavrentiy Pavlovich Beria, Stalin's feared chief of secret police, sitting in back.

The next day we were, like every morning, at the beach. Next to us sat a very hairy man, a sort of orangutan. The man smiled at us, approached us, we introduced ourselves, and started to chat. We saw him again the next day and started the conversation where we had left off. He had a camera, we posed for him, sometimes he would pose for us, and we'd ask

**50** / Soviet Communal Living

a passer-by to take the picture. He wasn't that sympathetic but I wasn't too wary, these superficial contacts are part of being on vacation.

At the time, I was sometimes called to Germany where I performed surgery as one of the allied Soviet troops' medical team. One morning I was brought a telegram asking me to return to Moscow immediately. I made my way to the Gagra train station where I learnt that there were no tickets available.

Walking back toward the rest home, in a sullen mood, I met our newly acquired friend, whose name was Rafael Semenovich Sarkisov. He was in command of Beria's praetorian guard, something I obviously still didn't know. He said to me, "You seem very grim, Boris Mikhailovich, what's happened?" I explained my situation to him and he answered, "Don't worry, we will find you some train tickets."

The next morning, a black Volga[1] came to pick us up at the rest home. The chauffeur in a NKVD uniform asked me: "Are you Boris Mikhailovich Gershman? I have orders to drive you to Sochi."[2]

Once we got to Sochi, we went to the station and my uniformed man told the person in charge: "Put this comrade and his wife in such-and-such compartment, in such-and-such wagon." He did not have to repeat it.

Sleeping cars are usually situated at the middle of a train but this one was at the end, once again, I paid no attention to it. The train started off and around 11 p.m. there was a knock on the compartment's door. I opened it, slightly worried, to see our orangutan but this time in a colonel's secret police uniform. Later on during the NKVD trials, I found out that his nickname was "Beria's faithful dog."

"You all right?" he asked me, adding with a mysterious look, "We attached ourselves along the road." That was when I realized that an additional car had been attached to the rear of our train during the night.

The next morning, we stopped for a brief time in a station, and I got off to buy some pastries. Getting back into the car, I saw Beria standing on the steps. Extremely embarrassed, I did not know what to do and hesitated for a brief moment. Beria noticed me and said to me: "Excuse me, I'm blocking your way." He then reached out a hand, which I had to take, and helped me up.

I was terrified but at the same time I did not fully realize what it meant. The trip went on for two days, and Beria did not speak to us anymore. I saw him come and go in the corridor, preceded and followed by bodyguards. Sarkisov, he sometimes came to chat with us, what's more I confusedly thought that he liked my wife.

Two or three days after returning to Moscow to our communal apartment, I was getting ready to travel to Germany, when somebody rang for us at the door: two rings. It was Sarkisov, accompanied by two people carrying bags filled with sausages, pickles, and cognac.

I let them in, all the while asking myself how they had managed to find our address which I had scrupulously avoided telling them. I was 28 years old and naively did not think it was so easy to find someone.

Sarkisov seemed horrified by our living conditions. "How can you live in a hole like this? And with more than one family!" he exclaimed adding with a perverse smile, "Don't you worry, we will install you in an individual apartment on Gorky Street, near the Kremlin. We have a couple of dozen people to send to Siberia there. You will have your own four rooms for yourselves." At that moment I was already in a state of indescribable terror, feeling something enormous coming at me, and understood my helplessness.

"Oh you should not, Rafael Semenovich," I said. "We are quite fine here, my wife and I."

"Ta, ta, ta," answered the colonel. "This will be settled on Saturday. Lavrentiy Pavlovich (Beria) has invited you for lunch at his dacha and we can speak again about the apartment, you can no longer live here."

He filled my glass with cognac and was going for my wife's when I stopped him: "No, Rafael Semenovich, not for her."

"Why not?" asked Beria's bodyguard.

"Because she is five months pregnant," I answered.

Sarkisov went pale, his tone changed. Ten minutes later he had disappeared, and we never saw him again. Beria had no use for a heavily pregnant woman.

If my wife had not been pregnant, we would have gotten a four room apartment, and I doubtless would have been long dead. I was saved from certain death and my wife from rape, my son who today is 45 years old and a doctor in Los Angeles.

And we stayed for a long time in our kommunalka with no toilets or hot water.

After Stalin's death in 1953 and Beria's arrest in June of the same year, newspapers started publishing letters and articles relating Beria's sexual obsessions, his habit of choosing his "prey" while walking in the street, and it was then that I realized what had happened. Moreover, years later, I knew a woman by chance who had been forced to become Beria's mistress whom the state police apparatus had offered to house in an apartment belonging to the theater director Meyerhold[3] in exchange for her "services."

During his trial in December, my wife was extremely frightened of being implicated. She burnt all the photos Sarkisov had taken at the beach in Gagra.

I told my son Yuri this story when he turned 18.

CHAPTER 12

# The Ambulance, the Dead, and the Others

> The professor [...] enjoyed cloudberry tea and lived on Prechistenka in an apartment with five rooms, one of which was occupied by a dry little old lady, the housekeeper Maria Stepanovna, who looked after the professor like a nanny.
>
> —Mikhail Bulgakov. *The Fatal Eggs*

The private hotel had belonged to my family: naval engineers who had come from Germany during Peter the Great's era. As for me, Nathalie F., I lived with my parents, pottery artists, in Leningrad where both died during World War II. I was six years old then.

It was very hard to leave Leningrad at the time of the blockade. A friend of my mother's took me with her when she fled, without a doubt she saved me. I found myself in Moscow, sheltered by my great-grandmother who only had one single room of the old private hotel.

We were four in this room, my grandmother and my aunt who in order to earn a living worked as a typist in a ministry. This aunt later adopted me to receive additional living space.

My grandmother and my great-grandmother spoke French well. When I became a fashion designer and started working with our designer Slava Zaitsev,[1] who was just starting out then, they translated the letters that Christian Dior sent to him.

54 / Soviet Communal Living

The entire private hotel had been transformed into one single kommu-nalka, in the Taganka[2] district. On the second floor were the old servants' rooms, and downstairs were what had been the master's apartments.

In all, 12 families shared the two floors. Our room was 18 square meters. In the courtyard, the old laundry room, the stables, and the car-riage house were also occupied; people had been put up everywhere.

It would snow in this house, and it took them a long time to fix the roof. Snow fell in our room. I can still see the water frozen on top of the bed where my great-grandmother died.

Oil stoves were set on tables in the corridor. For many years, we did not have a kitchen. I would stay for hours in the corridor, which was dark but much warmer than our ice-cold room.

On the first floor lived Katia. The whole house called her the witch. Her room was near the exit, from her window she would spy and hurl abuse on everybody. She was in charge of collecting firewood and of watching the stove.

In this house I had been nicknamed "the ambulance," because I knew how to handle drunks. What's more, years later I ended up marrying one...There was a couple: he was a taxi driver and a compulsive drunk, and she was a hairstylist. One day, the woman called me, screaming, I came running, the man was very, very sick but I knew what to do. I heated his legs, put a cold compress on his heart, and gave him burning hot coffee with soda just as I used to do with Khokhol,[3] another alcoholic who also lived with us, who cleaned the floors in nightclubs.

She called me a second time, but it was too late. He had drunk a whole bottle of vodka, practically in one gulp, had had a spasm and had become purple. I could not even open his mouth, his teeth were clenched so tightly. His wife kept screaming. I yelled for her to go get a doctor and started massaging the drunk's neck to make the spasm go away, when all of a sudden I felt him stiffen. He was dead and when the ambulance, the real one, arrived, it was all over.

There was also a blind couple in the kommunalka: Marivanna and Ivan Ivanovich. They worked putting caps on bottles in an alcohol factory. Both drank a lot. Every day they'd steal some vodka from the factory and pour it in a condom they would attach to their legs. Marivanna told me about this one day when she was drunk.

At home, we would help them. In a communal apartment surrounded by stuff that does not belong to you, it is very hard for a blind person to recognize their own things. One day, Marivanna argued with one of the tenants in the kitchen: a little later she called me and said, "Natasha, what is in this bowl of soup?" I looked: the neighbor had emptied the basket filled with wastepaper and used matches into the blind woman's soup.

When they had been drinking, Marivanna and Ivan Ivanovich sang very, very loudly and clapped their hands. Then they inevitably would fight. Once Ivan chased after her down the corridor and the staircase with his axe[4] but the neighbors stopped him in time.

Diadia Iakov, another neighbor, was a floor sweeper in a train station. He was 75 years old when his first wife died. Shortly after, he married a woman of 45 from Tula[5] who only wanted to live in Moscow. Of course, he could not satisfy her, and she would tell everyone about it while preparing supper.

One night, they invited a man in a chauffeur's cap, who had procured vodka for them, for a drink. The old man quickly fell asleep and what had to happen between the other two happened.

But Iakov woke up and started shouting. The whole apartment came into the room in the middle of the night to find these three characters in a full-fledged fight. The guest had already torn off half of our poor old man's ear, and we had to call the police who took the hooligan to the station while an ambulance transported the old man to the hospital. Yakov came back soon after, saying, "She's fully capable of having others come around while I'm not here."

We also had our deported woman, a German, Laura Adolfovna, she was sent to Central Asia after the decree to expel Germans from Moscow. She was kind, always stroking my head and gave me candy. Some soldiers came one evening around 11, gave her two hours to pack her suitcase, and took her away. She was 70 years old.

An old religious woman who took in all the abandoned cats lived in the apartment. She had about 12 at home, in her room obviously; cats and dogs are not allowed in the corridor in a kommunalka, there's always a tenant who cannot stand them. This elderly woman had lived in a monastery before the Revolution.

One day she told me her story: her mother was an aristocrat who had cheated on her husband and had taken her vows with her daughters to expiate her sin. Antonina Ivanovna had never wanted to leave her mother; she had stayed in the monastery until the Soviet authorities closed it.

The walls of her room were covered with icons, some of great value. Two hours after her death all the icons had disappeared. The old ladies from church had stripped it bare.

I wrote my first letter to Stalin when I was nine years old, in 1944, to ask him for an apartment with a ceiling. I got this apartment in 1972, nearly 30 years later.

CHAPTER 13

# The American Legacy

> Ivanopulo's room was exactly the same size as Nicky's but, being a corner room, had one wall made of brick [...] Ippolit Matveyevich noted with dismay that he did not even have a mattress. "This will do nicely", said Ostap. "Quite a decent size for Moscow. If we all three lie on the floor, there will even be some room to spare."
>
> —Ilf & Petrov. *The Twelve Chairs*

My mother was born in the United States of an American father and a Russian mother of German/Jewish ancestry: my grandmother's name was Schinder. My maternal grandparents traded with Russia at the beginning of the century. Trade prospered between the two countries even after the Revolution. They specialized in the import/export of musical instruments.

In 1926, my grandmother and my aunt had come to Russia on business, bringing my mother with them who was 12 years old. But they went bankrupt and were prevented from leaving by the Bolsheviks. They settled in nearby Saratov where my mother, whose maiden name was Atlanta Provlay, grew up.

My mother is an extraordinary person. During the war she even was an airplane pilot; she studied at the Aviation Institute in Engels.[1] She then became a taxi driver in Saratov and stayed as such until her retirement. She still lives there today, she's 80 and hardly speaks English anymore.

## 58 / Soviet Communal Living

I, John S., was born in 1938 in Engels, capital of the Volga German Autonomous Soviet Socialist Republic.[2] We first lived with mother in a three-room communal apartment in Saratov where six of us lived in a room of 6 square meters. When I was seven, my father separated from my mother, and I came to live with him in Moscow. We found a room in a basement not far from the Soviet Army Theater. Before the Revolution, the place had been used as a warehouse for a business and had been transformed into a hospital during the war. It had been inhabited since the end of the war.

The set up was classical: six rooms, six families, a kitchen, and some toilets. No bathroom or hot water.

One of the rooms was occupied by a Jewish tailor and his wife from Belorussia with their two sons and their daughter. One of the son's was named Adolph; we renamed him Hitler.

Then there was Olga Fedorovna, the crazy woman. She never came out of her room—when her husband was drunk, she would literally kick him out, and he slept outside the apartment in the staircase.

Then came Marveevsky's room, a Polish shoemaker with three daughters. All four of them had tuberculosis. Contagious sick people are theoretically kept far from communal apartments but in this case apparently it didn't bother anyone.

My father remarried a woman who had a son two years younger than me. They lived with us. There were four of us already when my father's brother, who worked for the KGB, arrived. Since we didn't have an available bed he slept under the table. Sometimes he brought women over and slept with them. I could not really call the brief activity he engaged in "making love," it had a certain effect on me but I had loads of fun.

He stayed with us for three years, made us do our homework and put food on the table under which he slept.

On weekends all the inhabitants would get drunk and play the board game lotto.

I have good memories of the incredible mess reigning in the apartment. We raised chickens in the corridor, about 20 of them. And then we built a puppet theater, we gave shows and had a lot of fun.

On Sundays, we played football in the corridor. We were a lot of children, at least seven. Vetochka, my favorite, became a dancer at Bolshoi. Her mother was the manager of a shop, a relatively enviable position at the time because you could obtain products that were impossible to find.

It was hard to live in a basement of course, but one had to live somewhere and believe me, we were not the only ones! In the '50s, in the big cities of the USSR, there were still many semi-basement apartments, I knew some in Saratov and elsewhere.

On Saturday mornings we would go to the baths. That was where my father would start drinking. He drank so much on weekends, that on Sundays, he sometimes would get to the point of taking his brother's gun and shoot it in the air. The whole house would resonate. When he was drunk, I would go to sleep in the corridor, scared that he would shoot.

One day, with the other kids, we were playing with matches and set the curtains on fire, and it made a huge scandal.

One fine day, the crazy woman who never left her room and whose drunken husband had abandoned her, died. We didn't find out about it for a long time, maybe a month, because it always smelt a lot in her room and in the whole apartment because of the chickens…

With the other kids we would have a lot of fun making paper bombs: we would throw wet balls of paper on the ceiling, they'd stick to it, and once they were dry they'd fall into saucepans, it was very funny. To go out into the courtyard, we would jump out of the kitchen window.

In 1956, we were given a room in a two-room apartment on Kutuzov Prospect,[3] thanks to my mother-in-law who was a party member and who was a secretary in one of the party organizations. I was studying mechanics at the Bauman Institute at the time, I was learning to inspect locomotive engines.

When she was young, my mother received money from her father in America. One day, a message came that her father had died, and that she had inherited a big sum, I think a real fortune in fact. My father who still lived with her in Saratov at the time was summoned by the NKVD and spent six months in prison. "You are a spy, what is this money you receive from abroad?," they asked him. They let him go in the end, when they understood he was not a secret agent at all, and that they had no chance of getting the money.

Out of all this affair, my mother only kept insurance receipts, $25,000 apiece. Much later, we tried investigating what they were, but the leads that we have are very tenuous, I have an incomplete bank account number, and I do not have the exact addresses of the heirs in the United States. I think they probably do not have the slightest wish to know if my mother and I still exist and couldn't care less about our communal lifestyle.

CHAPTER 14

# Jewish Poison in the Pots

> The apartment had been quiet when Varya had arrived. At nine, the place came to life, with voices and footsteps in the corridor and doors slamming. Vika paid no attention to any of it. Everyone lived his own life here, everybody minded his own business, not even Vadim bothered to look in.
>
> —Anatoly Rybakov, *Children of the Arbat*

I was born in Samarkand[1] to a Jewish family from Uzbekistan: the Katzs. My father was an expert in wine production. He had a diploma from the Imperial Botanical Nikitski Institute in Yalta and had done an internship in France at the beginning of the century. He was 22 years older than my mother, a theater actress.

In Samarkand, we lived in a big house all by ourselves. In 1946 however, we came to live in Moscow to be closer to my sister, who was studying voice at the Conservatory of Leningrad, and also because my father was having problems in Central Asia. Arrested in 1924, he had been accused of being a dirty capitalist and of hiding gold and jewelry. It was true; it is, in fact, thanks to those jewels that he was set free, handing them over on the sly to the Procurator.

In 1937, he was once again arrested in Samarkand. The director of the wine factory had accused him of being a spy for Estonia and of preparing an attack on the factory. Why Estonia, is still a mystery today. He was in prison for a year and when he came out, on May 10, 1938, he decided first to leave for Tashkent,[2] then for Moscow.

In Moscow, father succeeded in being transferred to an Uzbek wine bottling factory, but we had no place to live. A nephew of my father's, the playwright Alexander Shtein, gave us his room in a communal apartment, in the cul-de-sac Ordynsky near Piatnitskaia Street, a pre-Revolutionary residential and commercial neighborhood. It was a beautiful apartment and our 28-square-meter room had a lot of light. It would have all been perfect, if only my family had not had to share this lodging with 18 other people . . .

One of the rooms was inhabited by Olga Nikitina, a typical Russian woman. She came from the country and remained a true peasant even after living in Moscow her whole life. The city only taught her how to swear. She always swore, probably not realizing how vulgar her speech was. She had a daughter, Tonia, same age as me, a son Slava, and a lover whom she called "Kobel," literally "male dog." This term is also used in Russian to describe a man who's sexually obsessed.

She was fat and looked like a balloon that had been tied in the middle. Her incredible kindness was only equaled by her vulgarity. She addressed her daughter as "the whore."

My father at first thought that Kobel was his surname . . . We were the only ones with a TV, and Olga would come every day to our room to sit in front of it. Ballet shows were very common at the time. When she saw the tutus on the screen she would scream in admiration and make comments: "But where are you sticking your leg? You ought to be ashamed of yourself."

I was about 12 years old. Olga took the role of a maid for my family. She would wash the corridor and the bathroom when it was our turn[3] and would do my mother's shopping.

The phone was in the corridor and when I started having suitors, I would cover it with a handkerchief so that they wouldn't hear her swearing.

A large family occupied two other small rooms. The mother lived with two daughters, one of which was married to a drunk. I do not remember ever seeing him sober. His young wife was terribly skinny, which didn't prevent her from bringing a baby into the world every year. She had five offspring of an alcoholic: skinny, pallid, with twisted legs, sickly.

It was impossible to enter into their rooms. As soon as they opened the door, a horrendous stench of urine, alcohol, dirty laundry, and unwashed children invaded the corridor. It was frightening. You had to see my mother, so distinguished and obsessed with cleanliness, going through the corridor. It was sheer torture for her.

Olga often prepared fruit syrup in a stockpot, in big quantities because she loved drinking some from time to time. She drank very noisily, it was interesting for me, I had been brought up in such a different way, I would then go tell mother everything.

Olga began noticing that her fruits in syrup were disappearing a bit too fast. So one day she threw a pack of laxatives into the pot and waited for what would follow. The next day, the family with five children was on the toilet from dawn on—they all had diarrhea. Scared to death, they knocked on Olga's door and cried out, "Olga, Olga, what did you put in your syrup?"

Olga then opened the door and with her hand on her hip and a radiant smile, said to them: "And what business is it of yours what I put in my fruits, I ask you!"

In the kitchen there were four tables, two refrigerators, one sole sink, and one single stove for everyone. The bathroom was constantly encumbered with bins of laundry and drying clothes. The toilets were practically inaccessible, always occupied, mainly by the five children of the alcoholic, then by Olga's Slava, and then by another Slava who had a wife and a child.

My father called this other Slava "Kostikum banditum." When he was drunk he would beat his wife with such violence that we would plug up our ears. She died young, and he remarried a stout woman whom he did not spare either. We'd never get involved, it wasn't any of our business except when he whipped his son, my father couldn't stand it, he would go knock on the wall and beg him to stop. And Kostikum would answer, "Shut your face, intelligentsia."

There were four bells installed on the front door, and he would always ring ours for a very long time when he came home drunk. His second wife would understand it was him and would run to open the door but he would push her away: "L-l-let intelligentsia c-come and o-open th-the door f-for me," he'd say.

The hardest was for my mother who had abandoned the stage and was often at home. She suffered terribly from this promiscuity, this vulgarity,

**64** / Soviet Communal Living

this dirt. My father, he too was miserable, he was very polite and would say hello to everybody but he could not converse with anyone and was forced to put up with all these louts.

We lived near the Tretiakov State Gallery.[4] Every Saturday and Sunday, father would take me by the hand, and we would go visit an exhibit. He explained everything to me—I knew the gallery inside and out. I still remember which paintings were in which rooms.

Twice a week we would go wash at the Kadashev baths,[5] very handily situated just in front of our building. My mother took diluted magnesium with her to wash and disinfect the toilets. Olga Nikitina came with us. She would go fetch hot water in a ewer from the room at the end because my mother could not stand really hot steam, she'd suffocate. The other inhabitants went to the baths less often than us, the children were washed in the kitchen.

Stalin was important to me. If I went to Red Square and he was not there, I would make a fuss. Not surprising that when the "Jewish doctors affair" exploded in 1948,[6] I reacted like everyone else at first. Coming home from school one day, I told my father that for the first time in my life I was ashamed to be Jewish. "For the first time in my life I am ashamed that you are my daughter," was his only answer. We never spoke about that episode again.

At the time newspapers were publishing satirical serials where the characters that were ridiculed had Jewish surnames, were bandits, speculators, and so on. Kostikum banditum took one of these papers, underlined all the Jewish names in it in red, and then put it on our kitchen table.

Because it was a state-mandated antisemitism, and therefore obligatory, everyone started treating us very badly. Everyone but Olga.

The family with five children, for example, decided to tie up all the handles of their pots to prevent us from pouring poison in them. Since Jewish doctors had poisoned the country, we could do as much in the apartment... One day, my mother was in the kitchen and one of the five children locked himself by mistake in our room, and the door could not be opened, not from the inside or from the outside. The child was crying and his mother started shouting: "You dirty Jew, you want to take my son's blood to make your unleavened bread!" According to an old anti-semitic Muscovite craziness, Jews used baby's blood to make unleavened bread. Why blood to make bread, is a mystery!

That evening my mother cried in our room all night long.

This was in 1949, we were harassed on a daily basis by the newspapers. My father said to my mother, "Do not pay attention, all this will pass." I have to say, the inhabitants of our apartment were louts but not informers. We were not scared.

When Stalin died, the whole apartment sobbed, except my father. Even my mother cried. Arguments stopped for a certain time, the Soviets were really lost, thrown into disarray.

I started working as a theater director in 1962. When I finished Gittis,[7] I still lived in my kommunalka. Then I met my future husband, an actor, and we moved to Kuibyshev.[8] We lived there in a kommunalka that we shared with a director and a lawyer. Totally different, it felt like living in a family.

We came back to Moscow in 1964, still in our old kommunalka but not for very long.

We received an apartment pretty fast: a three-room Khrushchoba[9] where we settled down with my father and my mother, my sister and her husband. Even though space was tight, we were all one family, it is a completely different story. All my life I will be thankful to Khrushchev for understanding that communal apartments had to end. The problem was far from being solved but at least 70 percent of our population was no longer living under these conditions as was the case up until the sixties.

CHAPTER 15

# The Letter

> "Are you the people they've moved into Fyodor Pavlovich Sablin's apartment?"
>
> "We are," confirmed Shvonder.
>
> —Mikhail Bulgakov. *Heart of a Dog*

I have spent my entire life in this apartment. I am 75 years old now. We first lived here with my father, my mother, and my sister. Then came my sister's husband, then mine, then the children were born, and we were still in these two little rooms. Then the parents died, then the husbands, then my sister... Today, I am alone. Well, alone here in my two rooms because THAT ONE, the policeman, chief commissioner at the Kazan train station, lives at the end of the corridor with his family and haunts me.

The other two rooms of the apartment are empty—the first because the woman who was registered there died before her daughter could register, it has been sealed up for years, the other one because the occupant recently took all his furniture God knows where, and we do not know who is going to show up.[1]

Up until 1950, there were about a dozen of us living here, now there are only four, but it is hell.

My father was the director of a branch of the People's Commissariat of Communications,[2] he was executed in 1937, denounced by one of our co-inhabitants who revealed that he was a noble and therefore an "enemy of the people." He was taken away on August 31st of that year, I remember

**68** / Soviet Communal Living

it because school was starting the next day, I was going into Grade 10.[3] I was 18 or 19, a little behind scholastically because I had been very ill during my childhood.

Three men rushed in during the night. They crossed the first room where I slept with my sister, I jumped up and I screamed, "What's happening?"

"Nothing, nothing, sleep," they answered. They did not search much, only my father's little desk. They left with him, my father told us: "All this is absurd, don't worry, I will be back soon." We never saw him again.

We searched for him in every jail, my mother and I, but in vain, we did not find him. Thousands of people disappeared in the same way during those years of terror.

An "Old Bolshevik" lived in the apartment,[4] with his special cards for provisions, a little sickly being, illiterate. He worked at the People's Communications Committee, the ministry where my father held the highest office.

He registered a complaint against me in 1949. We appeared in front of a People's Court, or Court of First Instance, where he alleged that I had beaten him with an iron bar, which caused him to develop pleurisy. The link between the two is not an obvious one but that is what he said.

In any case I knew that as the daughter of an enemy of the people nobody would defend me. Back in 1941, my mother had been arrested, again thanks to the same fellow, but at the time I didn't yet know it was him.

In any case somebody had denounced her, because a prosecutor had come to the house, and my mother had been called in the very next day and then committed to a psychiatric asylum, which was apart of the prison of Matrosskaia Tishina for two months.[5] My mother told me how they made her immerse herself in a bath filled with icy cold water every day. Two months later she had dropsy, they brought her home where she died some weeks later.

But in 1949, the year of my trial, something incredible happened. I was in the kitchen where we had a wastebasket specifically for paper, which we then burned in the stove. To remove a burning hot dish out of the oven, I grabbed a bit of crumpled paper from the wastebasket, and I unfurled it to get a better hold of the dish, That was when I saw my married name, Volkov—my first husband's name. The letter was signed by Mikhail Pavlovich N., the Old Bolshevik.

I took the crumpled paper to my room, and I reconstructed the letter, which was a draft. As soon as I read it I was gripped by an indescribable fear, understanding who had killed my father and without a doubt my mother, and with whom I had been sharing a bathroom and kitchen since my childhood. I sent everything to the Central Party Committee, which didn't file suit, obviously, on behalf of the daughter of an enemy of the state...

Here is the text of that letter:[6]

> To the Ministry of State Security of the USSR, from a member of MKPB (Moscow Committee of the Bolshevik Communist Party).
>
> The inertia of local branches of the ministry of Security, within the Red Guard district, in view of the impudence of enemies of Soviet authority,
>
> [...] give the neighbourhood a feeling that forces of order are incapable of fighting enemies of the Soviet State, and forces me to address the following declaration to you:
>
> In apartment number 76 on Solianka Street, live two sisters, Stepankova and Volkova, born Sosnovsky. Their father Sosnovsky, a lawyer of noble origin, used to live in this house and was exposed in 1937 as an enemy of Soviet authority for having corresponded in 1935, 1936 and 1937 with the Germans.
>
> But this is not a matter of their heritage but rather their behaviour as a lethal enemy of Soviet authority since their father's denunciation. At the beginning of the war, in 1941, Volkova was evacuated to the Cheliabinsk region[7] with her two-year-old son. In October, during the most difficult days, when the enemy was at the doors of the capital, Volkova returned to Moscow and openly threatened the whole apartment, saying: "You will see, when the Germans are here, we will settle our debts, and we will take revenge for what you did to our father."
>
> Why local authorities hesitate to accost citizen Volkova for such acts, I cannot understand. But personally, I think that secret enemies have to be rendered hamless and neutralized.
>
> Not only does Volkova terrorize me, even though I am not easily scared, but she recently, in the kitchen, took a metal bar and hit me in the chest. I couldn't work for two weeks after that. All this because I exposed her father.

I am not addressing myself to you for physical damages, I brought suit in front of the tribunal which will render judgement itself. It's also not a personal matter. No, I only ask myself why an enemy of Soviet authority can act with impunity within the capital, under the eye and knowledge of this same power.

I who am an Old Bolshevik, I cannot explain how a non-Party person can tranquilly live in our apartment. I think something must be done so that she can no longer be threatening nor even hold her head high.

Please excuse me for bothering you. The affair's files can be found at the Ministry of the Interior's station for the Red Guard district, where they were sent by the Moscow MVD department of the same district.

Signed: N., employee of the Ministry of Communications since March 1917, Party card number XXXXXXX. April 1949.

After this drama, I had to continue living with him, sharing the same kitchen and the same bathroom. Impossible to move out. Who in Moscow would want two adjoining rooms, with just one exit door onto the corridor?[8] If they had had separate doors maybe, but in our case, there was never any candidate, we searched for a while, we even paid someone to do this. Then it became too expensive and pointless so we gave up.

After having sent a copy of this letter to the Central Commitee, the Party called me in December 1949. They told me they had interrogated N., and that he was not able to deny it since his Party card number was on it. But N. had assured them that it was not him who had written but another inhabitant of the apartment, a Jew who was a letter writer. N., he had only signed it!

It was all the more ridiculous since the Jew only wrote under dictation and since N. was illiterate. But for the Party, the explanation was sufficient to close the file and exculpate the prosecutor. The only positive result: N let lapse the complaint against me for "blows and injuries."

CHAPTER 16

# New Year's Eve Celebration

> Everyone who lived in the communal apartment had his own way of coming in. Galya slammed the door and rushed down the corridor. Mikhail Mikhailovich came in quietly, delicately, almost without being detected.
>
> —Anatoly Rybakov. *Children of the Arbat*

What I preferred were parties, especially New Year's celebrations. The house was immense, 13 rooms, it was an old private hotel built by my grandmother's husband after the communists took everything from us. My great-grandfather, German and noble, owned two entire streets: Bolshaia and Malaia Ekaterinskaia.

The building became communal quite late—in 1940 when I was born, it was still a private residence. My mother and my grandmother told me about the maids' rooms, the big orchard, and that they went horseback riding in Piatigorsk.[1] It sounded like a fairytale to me: I would imagine them riding like Amazons, dressed in their crinolines.

We were evacuated from Moscow during the war, and when we came back—my father died at the Front—the house was occupied, and we were only left with two rooms. And what rooms at that... A piece of shrapnel had fallen on the roof, the ceiling was half collapsed, it snowed in the house.

My mother and my grandmother worked, and there were already three of us children. We had many friends of our age. Each room had two or three children living in it, and since the parents were all working, we had a lot of freedom.

The adults would make extraordinary efforts for New Year's Eve. We put Christmas trees in each room.[2] We would make Christmas decorations ourselves and gather in the kitchen to paint and hang them.

I also remember Easter which was prohibited but all the inhabitants except for one followed the Orthodox tradition. The man who did not celebrate worked in the Special Services, but at home he never interfered in other people's habits. His family didn't talk to us but it did not bother us too much, we paid no attention to it.

We would prepare the Kulichi[3] in the kitchen. Kulichi and vanilla odors inevitably evoke in me these very happy childhood times. We would paint Easter eggs and then hide them in the old orchard, which had become a wild grove.

We would knock on doors, asking "Do you have an onion?," or flour or salt. Doors were rarely closed, we lived in a community.

During New Year's Eve, the grownups danced in the corridor, and then we sang a lot.

Then, bit by bit relationships grew strained, people started growing jealous. One of the neighbors would buy china, which she'd resell at a higher price in the courtyard. It was "speculation," totally prohibited, but the boldest people knew it was the best way to get rich. This neighbor began living better than the others. In the kitchen we could see what she would prepare for her family. They were undeniably richer than us, that was the beginning of the jealousy, there was underlying aggression in conversations.

Progressively, doors were closed. First with keys, then with locks, individual doorbells were installed on the front door. This was in the '50s, the inhabitants started blocking the doors on the inside with a wooden plank, after 11p.m. nobody could come into the apartment.

All communal accommodations had a system that allowed you to see if all the tenants were in, for example, little numbered plaques, which each person would hang on a board when they came back home, so that the front door would not be locked if some tenants were still out.

In 1963, a tenant complained against me. It was our turn to wash the corridor. It was Saturday, I was 23, and I desperately wanted to go to a party. My mother and my grandmother were ill or tired. After having scrubbed the parquet floor, I had an idea of covering the floor with newspapers,[4] to avoid the mass of inhabitants—who were mostly at the baths—from dirtying everything when they came back.

In a frenzy of activity, I cut a piece of newspaper to cover the toilet seat, I thought it would be more hygienic. I did not notice that Khrushchev's picture was at the bottom of the page, it would have been difficult to do otherwise because photos of our leaders were everywhere.

One of the inhabitants made a scene pretending that I lacked respect, that I had insulted the Politburo etc. She used to do my grandmother's laundry and was doubtless delighted to get revenge. Well, this woman went and denounced me to the building's committee, and her son registered an official complaint at the Dzerzhinsky area court. Thankfully, the judges were lenient and understood how ridiculous the whole affair was and contented themselves by letting me off with a warning. Had it been during Stalin's times, this would surely have ended very differently.

Aged 26, I couldn't stand living with my mother and all of these neighbors. I managed to get a room in a small three-room kommunalka. It was 1966, people started getting individual accommodations.

But one of the inhabitants was never there and the other, a bachelor my age, drank a lot. When he was drunk, he would knock on my door all night long. I was terrified. I would open the window and call the neighbors for help. I was scared, I was alone, so was he, and he was dangerous. But the Soviet authorities could not care less about such details; according to the authorities there was nothing abnormal, it was our "private life."

For single people like me, living in a kommunalka is even harder than for families, because there is the danger of being attacked at night by a neighbor, drunk or simply excited by the presence of a single young woman in one of the rooms.

I wandered from kommunalka to kommunalka for a long time. Different problems every time. In the '70s, I lived in a room in Bibirevo in a 3-room flat.[5] My room was huge and very pleasant. But my neighbor lived with her son, her mother, her future second husband, her dog, and her parrot. She then had another child. She only had these two tiny rooms for all these people, and she tortured me constantly repeating how unfair it was for me to have the prettier room.

It was an exhausting time for me. I would go to work in a factory in the very center of Moscow, taking a huge overcrowded bus, the ride took an hour and a half. The capital was full of "limitchiki" at the time; people were arriving from the most secluded areas of the USSR, to build

**74** / Soviet Communal Living

installations for the Olympics.[6] The mass of workers were everywhere. Imagine those buildings with so many floors, so many apartments, each room filled with an unbelievable amount of people.

The parrot drove me nuts. I still have an undying hatred for birds' singing. When I'm in the country, I can't stand it, their cooing gets on my nerves.

And then life in a kitchen which is so fundamental in this country is impossible in a kommunalka. I could not invite friends over, and I do not like receiving guests in my room. It is not the same. There is the bed, the cupboard, suitcases sticking out under the armchair,[7] all your personal life. In the kitchen, one can sit for a long time around the table to chat, drink, and sing…there, no.

Sometimes I even went to bed without eating because this woman did everything to drive me crazy. She pretended that because of her large family all was within her rights. "Evgenia can wait, she has ALL the time in the world," she would say. She would wash her laundry in the bathtub for hours, obviously not letting me in. In a kommunalka, while men can be dangerous for a single woman, mothers they are unbearable.

CHAPTER 17

# How Thirty People Can Share an Apartment

> A cry, stamping, a crack and various shouts resound in our communal apartment. The tenants rush to the scene, and this is what they see. The tenant Borka Fomin is meandering around his room in pink underpants.
>
> —Mikhail Zoshchenko. "A Tragicomedy"
> (*Nervous People and Other Satires*)

There were 30 of us, in 10 rooms. My family lived in a 10-square-meter room in which was enthroned a very high couch. My mother's first husband had a shop in Odessa, couldn't stand that it was expropriated during the Revolution, started drinking, and finally died under the wheels of a tram. Then my mother, paradoxically, married a staunch communist, who was a party member, which did not stop him from living in communal lodging. Only the Nomenklatura's top echelon escaped this fate.

The corridor was very long. Grusha, a woman working in a beer bar at the end of the street, was in charge of the apartment and terrorized all the inhabitants, especially the teacher and her son who had not spoken to anyone since the day the husband had disappeared. For us he just vanished, which is what sometimes happens, to men usually, who disappear for entire weeks but in fact he had been arrested. I found out much later

**76** / Soviet Communal Living

that he had found a way to earn a few dollars and that doubtless "Tiotia Grusha" had denounced him.

Neither the woman nor her son spoke in the kitchen, we knew almost nothing about them, it was a very secretive family. Whenever I went for a walk with my friends, we tried to see what was happening in their room because we lived on the ground floor.

Grusha came from the country. She boarded a "student" who paid her and who soon became her lover, an odd person but very intelligent. He then worked as a guard in the Kalinin Museum.[1] She also put up a niece who was in love with Arkady Raikin.[2] She would go to all his concerts and bought him bouquets of flowers that she threw on the stage.

One of the inhabitants was very pretty, her husband had been killed in the war, and she was very sought after. She would send her son to sleep at his grandmother's to allow her to have her lovers. She let them use the bathroom and the toilets, which infuriated Grusha.

The resident drunk in the apartment was a roofer; he had three daughters. His wife and he did not participate much in life at the apartment. He would come back late at night, completely drunk, his wife having paced up and down the corridor, ending up waiting for him on the porch, Grusha shouting because the entrance door remained open.

There was also a singer who in the beginning lived with her husband and her daughter. She was extremely cultured, constantly played the piano, and her daughter played the guitar. We called her Iolka.[3] Then her husband left and her daughter started distancing herself from her mother because she never prepared anything to eat.

She believed in God. We, we were afraid of religion. We knew that practicing it was prohibited,[4] and we had never been baptized. Even when we baptized our daughter, my husband and I, we didn't have any witnesses, out of fear of being denounced.

Iolka sang in the "Elokhovsky" church choir.[5] It was the beginning of the '50s. She did not talk about her faith but always invoked God and drew little crosses on the doors of our rooms at every religious celebration.

She was very discreet. She would go into the kitchen when nobody was there and would sing covering her mouth with her hand so as not to disturb anyone, I heard her because our room abutted the kitchen. She sang classical music, religious chants, requiems . . . it was beautiful. She lived in her own world, not paying attention to anyone but was very kind.

Iolka brought home abandoned cats, she'd feed them and then would leave them in the corridor. This often resulted in massive dramas because the cats would eat too much and then throw up and Grusha would shout that she was in charge of the apartment and that this scandal had to end.

Grusha was perhaps in charge but that did not prevent her from coming back drunk from work every day. She would bring back whole bags of coins. Her lover, who was called Shebek, would have to count them. They then bought a small TV, and they invited us to their room, not out of generosity but because they liked showing it off, as if they were rich.

She terrorized us, everybody was afraid to talk in her presence. The teacher would never say a word to her but their rooms were adjoining and doubtless Grusha heard things when the husband was still there.

The kitchen was filled with small, oil stoves and at 6 p.m.[6] they'd make noise and emit a terrible smell.

Grusha, she made her meals in her own room and never came to the kitchen. She ate much better than we did, but that didn't mean much according to the smell, cabbage soup and buckwheat porridge.

I remember the kitchen as a nightmare. The tap ran constantly and you had to put buckets everywhere because of leaks. The room was not heated and these puddles froze in the winter.

Our toilet shared a wall with that of the next kommunalka. The children amused themselves by making a hole through the wall and when you used the toilet, some kid from the other side would inevitably stick his finger in the hole or say, "I see you neighbor!" I never understood how Shebek could stay in there for hours; it was so cold that the water in the toilet bowl froze.

We stood in line in front of the toilets in the morning, those who went back to their room would miss their turn. We had chamber pots but it was not very practical, you still had to go out and empty it in the toilet.

Then German prisoners did some renovations in the house. They put in pipes and we had gas. Oil stoves were replaced by two kitchen ranges with four burners each. We would heat up the kitchen by simultaneously lighting the eight burners,[7] and then we started washing ourselves in the kitchen, which did not prevent neighbors from coming in—on the contrary.

We lived in this apartment until the '70s. I got married and studied at the Foreign Language Institute before joining the Faculty of Journalism.

## 78 / Soviet Communal Living

Despite the terrifying conditions in which we lived, we had good moments. For New Year's, we would dance in the corridor to the sound of a "patefon," we would all invite each other to this room and that room.

We even took the patefon out to the courtyard. Once, I put on a pair of high-heeled shoes my mother had received in the name of humanitarian aid from America and went down to the yard to show them off. They hurt my feet terribly, and I ended up throwing them into the stove.

In as much as toilet issues obsessed us, we never spoke of sex. We were brought up as if sex did not exist, and at the same time we lived in conditions of promiscuity that shattered not only ideological prudishness but what little natural instinct we still had.

So I'd ask myself: "How can it be that THEY cannot see that a person has to be individual, to please, to seduce." I was young, it is only today, after 50 years, that I realized that they understand only too well, and that they just saw us as a workforce, as cattle.

CHAPTER 18

# The Gulag and the Roslovian Smell

> At this point seven newspapers are brought in from various rooms. Everyone looks and checks, and they see that there's no doubt about it. Borka Fomin, a fellow with no pretensions to being anyone special, has won five thousand, and no one knows what he's going to do with the money.
>
> —Mikhaïl Zoshchenko. "A Tragicomedy"
> (*Nervous People and Other Satires*)

My father, Ivars Smilga, was a Latvian, a militant for the Russian Social-Democratic Workers Party[1] since 1907. He was one of the first members of the Central Committee of the Communist Party, commander of the Baltic fleet, the Army Council and the Helsinki fleet beginning in the summer of 1917. Lenin who was 22 years older than him, respected him deeply.

He was close to Trotsky, I remember Leon Trotsky with his wife at my parents, he was always interested in my sister and me, asked us questions. On the eve of the Revolution, Lenin wrote him a letter, that was only published much later, where he said that the time for the provisional government would not come by itself and that radical measures had to be taken.

My father came to Moscow to study at the University, he was arrested for the first time at 17 after Leo Tolstoy's death for having participated in demonstrations in favor of individual freedom.

**80** / Soviet Communal Living

After the civil war, he was appointed Director of the Central Department of Combustibles, and he was one of the founders of Gosplan.[2] After that he became the rector of the Economics Institute of Plekhanov University.[3]

He was also responsible for the program of the "Memoirs" publication of the Academia, which was the leading Soviet publishing house of that time.

But he was in the opposition. He was even one of its leaders at the 15th Party conference.[4] In 1927, the whole group made up of Trotsky, Kamenev, Zinoviev, my father, Rakovski, Preobrazhenski, warned against the advent of the terror and the construction of camps.[5] The opposition staff met in our apartment. We were living at the time in the "the House on the Embankment"[6] where all the members of the government lived.

It was too late. Stalin was already there. In 1928, my father was sent into exile for the first time. When he came back, he gave up on the opposition and changed his method, trying to use persuasion. He became head of the Supreme Economic Council, tried to convince Stalin to change the economic policy and to move on to khozrashchet.[7] All in vain, Stalin sent him to Tashkent in 1933.

Back from Central Asia in 1934, my father was unemployed for six months, constantly second-guessing himself, trying to understand what had happened. He was 41 years old. He was arrested on January 1, 1935, one month after Kirov's assassination.

My life all of a sudden practically stopped, I was 15 years old. They refused to allow us in the Komsomol,[8] threw us out of the "House on the Embankment" within a few days. My mother was expelled from the Party and lost her secretarial job at the Soviet Encyclopedia Publishing House. My father, he was taken away with his card—they didn't even bother with the farce of Party exclusion that they had used with others, notably Zinoviev and Kamenev.

This is when, for the first time in my life, I lived in a kommunalka on Gorky Street, after a childhood that was undoubtedly overly marked by happiness. When mother was taken away on July 1, 1936, "neighbors" arrived in the apartment. My sister and I shared the room with our nurse who never abandoned us.

A lot of nurses distanced themselves from the children of the victims of purges mainly because they were afraid that they in turn would be the targets of repression, and also because nobody paid them. But Anna

Kuzmichna, our nurse, came to visit my mother when my father was arrested, and even if she no longer worked for us—she was a seamstress in a theater, she said to my mother: "I will raise your kids, I do not need to be paid." She stayed with us after mother was taken away.

Life in that apartment was not too bad, I was young and I suffered the loss of my parents too deeply to notice anything else. Not knowing where my mother was drove me insane. I knew my father was in an "isolator."[9] We could write him and he could too, he'd tell us he was learning French and we sent him books. "Niania" was without a doubt the one who suffered the most from all the kitchen and communal bathroom goings-on. At the age of 16, I remember going round all the prisons, I tried to send mother the little money she had left—she had sold a gold watch and some silver objects.

We were not hungry, Niania fed us properly but I remember Sundays when neighbors prepared cakes in the kitchen, it would smell so nice in the whole apartment. I drooled. I discovered for the first time what it was like to want to eat and not to be able to, a sensation I would often experience afterward.

We lived like this from 1936 to 1939. Our relations with the neighbors were not bad, but life was very hard. First of all, no school admitted me, I wanted to do theater. I tried the Film Institute, same thing. I went from humiliation to humiliation. As soon as I mentioned that my parents were not there, people's expressions would change, rejection was a certainty.

So I decided to start studying French, Papa wrote us that when he returned from prison he would teach us all the French he had learned. I wanted to become a literary translator from French into Russian. I adore Mérimée.

One day, a cousin called me and said that a kid who had known me since childhood and whose parents had also been arrested wanted to see me. I was not suspicious. In fact, he had been instructed to watch me, it was very common among students; each group had its Judas. He was the one who denounced me; he reported that I'd always say worldwide revolution could not occur if all the Old Bolsheviks were put in prison. It was true, it was my obsession.

They came to get me one night at two in the morning. The neighbors were terrified, they were taking away a girl with no parents, my sister was sobbing. I was trembling with fear but I told her, "Natasha don't cry, I am

## 82 / Soviet Communal Living

20 already, that's already more than mother, she was 19 the first time she got arrested, don't cry Natasha." They were there, standing in the room, two men and a driver, and they did not even turn around when I had to take off my nightgown to get dressed.

I was taken to the Lubianka prison,[10] where I spent three months. Then three more in Butyrki,[11] after which I was sent to a camp in Mordovia.[12] That night, the "organs"[13] arrested five other girls from my class. They accused us of being a subversive group when we were not even friends, other than one. The charge was a major one and made reference to articles 58, 10, and 11. 10 was propaganda, 11 is for the group. In other words, I was likely to attack the Kremlin, me who lived for the theater, who only dreamed of living with my parents and studying.

The doors of the Lubianka slammed closed behind me. Still today, I can't even walk by the building.

I was sentenced by three men to three years in a labor camp, without even having a trial in front of a tribunal. In fact, I actually spent four years and four months in the Gulag. At the end of three years, I was not freed because the war started. I slept outside the camp but worked just as much.

When they let me go, one year and four months later because of my legs—inherited from my father, an illness which was aggravated in the Gulag—I had to live another 13 years far from Moscow; I was forbidden to come back. Because of articles 38 and 39 of the Penal Code, I could not even spend a night in the capital.

I was rehabilitated in 1956—my father only in 1987, 50 years after his death. In the 17 wasted years of my life, the administration only counted the three years in the gulag, and last year gave me a financial compensation of 24,000 rubles. I recently paid 16,000 rubles to fix my teeth, so I spent 2/3 of my Gulag compensation at the dentist's.

We never saw Niania again. She died, alone, in the communal apartment in Moscow, during my exile in Riazan.[14] My sister, she is still somewhere else, in a city where she was exiled 10 years after me. Neither of us two could go back to be with her.

After Stalin's death, I finally received a "clean" interior passport in 1954. I left for Moscow immediately, legally, but had no accommodation. I first rented a room in an apartment near Moscow, with walls so thin you could hear everything. When my 3-year-old daughter, Svetlana, fell ill, I would beg her not to cry for fear of getting kicked out of our refuge. It was more a corner than a room, really.

I lived there with my little daughter until 1956. I have good memories of it because I followed the 20th Congress from there.[15] It is hard for me to explain how happy I was to hear on the radio that all those who had been arrested were not guilty. I was 36, had had no news from my parents for 20 years, but was convinced at the time that they were still alive. I was quickly disappointed; both had been dead for ages.

I lived in an irregular situation. I no longer had a "propiska"—the registered permission to live in Moscow. It had been annulled after my arrest 15 years earlier. In order to receive lodging, that is to say an actual room in a kommunalka where I could live regularly, I needed one.

In 1958, I finally received the authorization to settle in a 14-square-meter room, in the Lenin hills, 18 Lomonosov Perspective. Rykov's daughter, Bukharin's daughter, and Tukhachevski's three sisters[16] also got lodging in that building. There was also a gipsy colony.

My "kingdom" was in a four-room apartment. In one room lived a couple with their daughter, and in the other two lived a family of 11 people, 8 of whom lived there permanently. Therefore we were, with Svetlana's father who had divorced and had come to join us, 17 people registered in the apartment.

Of course, everybody shared a single bathroom and a single 9-square-meter kitchen and used the toilets after lining up in the corridor.

The first alarm clock rang at 5 a.m., and the last neighbor to be in bed would switch off the light around 2 a.m. It was like a train station. I who have bad nerves since the Gulag and suffer from insomnia, I could only really sleep two hours per night. They didn't know how to close that toilet door softly, even when there were "only" eight—try counting how many times that door would slam.

My room was near the kitchen, the toilets, and the bathroom. When cabbage was cut in the kitchen, my bed was just on the other side, I would hear chak-chak-chak-chak. It was Katia. She was not working and liked to rest all day, only to get active around 10 at night. She preferred doing her laundry at night, and Zhzhzhzhzhzh... the water would run in the bathroom, behind our walls that were so thin that you couldn't put a nail in the wall without everything falling apart. And then *slam!* the toilet door would open and *slam!*, the toilet door would close...

It was impossible to sleep. And if, exhausted by not getting any shut-eye, I wanted to get up early in the morning, around six, impossible to use the bathroom even for a short while. "Tania, you do not have to go to

**84** / Soviet Communal Living

work, so please be kind, come back in two hours when we've left." I did not have the right to wash up before 9 in the morning.

The father was always drunk but he was nice and constantly apologized. "I-I love you and I respect you, f-forgive me for being drunk," he would hiccup. I would say to him, "I beg you, Vasily Ivanovich, drink, but please stop apologizing."

They had two sons, Boria and Volodia. Just back from the army, they got married and procreated straight away. From 11, they became 15 in two rooms. One of them, I don't remember if it was Boria or the other one, was a handsome fellow, sang "Les grands boulevards" and "C'est si Bon," while strutting down the corridor: Yves Montand[17] had visited Moscow, he was the idol of the younger generation. He also sang a very popular song, "Le Temps des Cerises,"[18] you know it goes "tararara-tararara-rara," I couldn't listen to it any more, I would plug my ears as soon as he'd start singing.

Of the 24 hours in a day, 3 would be calm. Sometimes during the summer, they would leave to go swimming in the Moskova,[19] I would open my door for an hour or two, and I'd relish the silence. For an hour I was happy, it was rare.

I sometimes tried talking to Katia, but she could not understand, it wasn't important to her that there was a blissful paradise that existed in the world, which is called silence. They were simple people, who did not consider music, peace, smells important to an individual's life.

Smells... oh the smells of that apartment... Still today, we talk about the "Roslovian smell" with my daughter when we enter an apartment that stinks. Roslov, it was their family name.

It is a smell of old dirty clothes, old shoes, unwashed bodies, a very interesting and very particular smell, hard to imagine for those who have never entered a kommunalka. But as soon as you cross the threshold of one of those apartments, the smell gets you.

Smells are fundamental to me, they represent my whole childhood. It's often the case, but for me in particular, because my childhood was happy as the following events were not. Mother adored perfumes, she had some very good ones and when my parents slept I would go to the bathroom and I would put some behind my ears before going to school. I was eight years old.

When I was in the Gulag and I slept on a straw pallet, there were no bad smells. The prisoners were women of total dignity, admirable. In the morning, we were given a washbasin with lukewarm water to use. The guards would give us a small bit of soap and each person would diligently wash and would scrub their lingerie. It was a question of survival; it was to endure interrogations, humiliation, vexation, to keep your head high. In the kommunalka, I am sorry to say, it stinks. There is no other way of saying it.

There was also the kitchen, with its constant smells of fried onion, of cabbage. I do like onion but when mixed with cabbage it does not smell very good, especially if the meal is not for you. One of the neighbors liked fried kambala,[20] she was my good friend, a smart woman, sensitive, refined, and cultured, the one who lived with her husband and her daughter. But frying Kambala emits, God knows why, a smell of sheep's wool. I slept next door—the unpleasant smell would spread in the corridor and accumulate in my room.

But the worst are clothes and shoes, you Westerners could not understand because you don't wear shoes until they are bursting from all seams, basically never changing socks.

These stories should be told to a doctor. Our way of life has had a fundamental influence on our collective psyche, that's why we are all sick because of the constant displacement of populations, of people, and then those terrifying promiscuities.

I have recurrent dreams: sometimes I see "the house on the bank" the only place where I was really happy, as a child. I sometimes dream of my father, of arrests on Tverskaya Street...Sometimes I dream of the gulag. But sometimes I also dream that I'm offered a room in a kommunalka in exchange for my actual little studio. In the dream I accept, because it is closer to my daughter. Then all of a sudden I realize the unforgivable error I have made and say to myself: "But what have you done? You've created yet another tragedy for yourself, and this time it's your own doing."

CHAPTER 19

# Ballad of a Soldier

> And he describes events not from the planet Mars, but from our accursed little earth, from our eastern hemisphere, where there just happens to be, in a certain building, a communal apartment in which the author resides.
>
> —Mikhail Zoshchenko. "The lilacs are blooming"
> (*Nervous People and Other Satires*)

I defended Stalingrad, I was injured four times in war and am one of the 240 survivors of a division of 14,000 men.

But I am also and before anything else, a film director. I've directed seven full-length features and four documentaries and write all the scripts for my films mysef, I, Grigory Naumovich Chukhrai.[1] *41*, my first important film, was selected at the Cannes Festival in 1957 or 1958 where it received a prize for "exceptional artistic quality, humanism and script originality." It was given a prize about a dozen times at international festivals.

My best known full-length feature is *Ballad of a Soldier,* which received a special jury prize in Cannes in 1960. It was the year *La Dolce Vita* received the Golden Palm. I cannot remember how many awards I received for this film anymore, newspapers mentioned about a hundred. It was even selected for the Festival of Festivals in San Francisco. I shot it in 1959, and at first had several problems with this work. In the USSR, it was considered ideologically subversive, and it could only be shown in the countryside and small villages, not in cities.

## 88 / Soviet Communal Living

I was temporarily expelled from the Party because of *Ballad of a Soldier* . The film was considered as slanderous of the Soviet Army. But the *Komsomolskaia Pravda*[2] newspaper published the result of a survey that showed that it was extremely popular with the public. The author of the article was the journalist Adzhubei,[3] Nikita Krushchev's son-in-law who advised his father-in-law to see it. Khrushchev watched it and appreciated it, and soon after the film was sent to Cannes.

In the USSR, this film won me the Lenin's Prize in 1962, and my Party card was returned to me. But *Ballad of a Soldier* was already a success around the world.

I had always dreamed of attending the Film Institute in Moscow. I had successfully passed my entry exams at the Institute, but I did not know where to live. Since the war, I had a piece of shrapnel in my lungs, when I coughed I spat blood, and I was asked to leave my "obshchezhitie"[4] because of fear of tuberculosis. What's more, I ended up contracting it a little later on.

In the meantime, my son had been born and my wife had left Ukraine where we had lived previously to come join me in Moscow. I weighed 54 kilos then, everybody was telling me to give up the Film Institute. I did not want to and stuck with it, with the help of some of my professors.

I needed to find an apartment. I found rooms one after the other in kommunalkas, but I did not have a "propiska," the police registration. Somebody denounced me every time, the police would come and chase me out. At the time, in all the building's inner courtyards there were one or two men whose job was to alert the police that there were unregistered new inhabitants.

We slept where we could, sometimes even in train stations.

I finally found a room where the police was agreeable that I settle in with my wife and child.

But at the KGB where I had to get a stamp of approval on a form, the official was of a different opinion altogether: "Unfortunately, I cannot authorize you to receive a propiska." I was distraught. "Why not?" I asked, almost in tears. "Because, my good man, it's not permitted to have just *anybody* living here." I got angry, I insisted, I reminded him of my wounds, Stalingrad, voice rising.

I got nothing. I was at my lowest point when I came out of there, walking in the streets looking at all the windows above of my head and meditating on the absurdity of life. I was walking like this down Gorky

Street, lost in my thoughts, when a black car stopped,[5] an officer got out of it and walked toward me. I thought straight away they were coming to arrest me after the argument with the KGB official. The man says to me: "The general wants you in the car." I thought it was the end. That they were going to arrest me.

It was in fact an officer I had known during the war, he told me: "I recognized you, how are you?" I explained to him that I had no place to live, and he decided to do something for me. He lived in "the House on the Embankment" and invited me to his place for a drink and promised me that he'd do something.

Arriving home, I had already been summoned by the police. There, it was explained to me that all my problems derived from my Ukrainian passport. Ukraine having been occupied by the Germans, was in disgrace, and all who had lived in an occupied zone could not be registered in Moscow.

They gave me a different internal passport thanks to which I first found a room in a basement. I could see passersby's legs from the window but I was happy. One day my three-year-old son was playing in the courtyard when he saw my wife cooking in the kitchen and said to her, "Mother, what are you doing down there? How did you manage to fall in that hole?" It was a big apartment, all the rooms were filled with people, some rooms even had two families in them.

Still, the atmosphere was rather pleasant. During celebrations we would invite each other to drink vodka. We lived normally in abnormal conditions.

It was a difficult time. In film school, Sergei Iosifovich Iutkevich,[6] my protector, was blacklisted as part of the campaign against cosmopolitism. He had written a book about Charlie Chaplin, and during a reunion in school, the Party had decided he was cosmopolitan. "Why write about Chaplin and not one of our own directors?" they said.

One day, a debate about the close-up exploded. "Who invented the close-up then? They say it's Griffith, it is not true, Kuleshov[7] did," said someone. And Kuleshov, terrified, answered, "No, no, it is not me." Close-ups were considered as traditionalist, and Kuleshov was terrified of being judged as such himself. These scenes were absurd but they were frequent.

Meanwhile, my health was considerably better. The piece of shrapnel had come out of my lung, and they were able to operate and remove it. I was still living in my basement.

**90** / Soviet Communal Living

Mikhail Ilyich Romm,[8] the new director of the Film Institute, then offered me work as an assistant director. I helped him a lot to shoot scenes in Crimea, I was very good at organizing battle scenes, I had the experience of war.

I finished my thesis, I went back to Ukraine, leaving my humid basement. Part of our group were Mark Donskoi[9] and Sergei Paradzhanov,[10] an absolutely extraordinary character capable of surprising gestures. One day at the station, he "borrowed" a bouquet of flowers from an official who was part of a delegation to meet someone, and temporarily offered the bouquet to my wife Irina who was getting off the train. He then gave it back to the official who looked completely taken aback . . .

Despite it all, I was not doing anything interesting. While in Ukraine, I received a telegram from the director of Mosfilm,[11] summoning me to Moscow for talks. He asked me if I'd like a permanent job in Mosfilm. I accepted.

That is how I came back to Moscow. Mosfilm's director, Ivan Alexandrovich Pyriev,[12] helped me obtain a room in an apartment not far from the studios. I then had my wife come.

This kommunalka only had two rooms, in the second room lived a family where the man was a chauffeur. My son was 11 in 1955 when we moved in, it was my first real room.

I had no furniture, I had put a mattress on the floor. We only had a little bed and a cupboard for Pavlik, my son, even though my mother and her husband were living with us. However, the room opened onto a balcony, plus at 35 years old for the first time in my life, I had a bathroom.

Therefore, I was happy but I could not work on my script during the day because there were too many people in the room.

So, when night fell, I would go in the bathroom, put a board on the bathtub and I worked. In the kitchen, the smell of food would disturb me, and then the neighbors could come in at any moment, it didn't happen that often in the bathroom.

We tried to keep on friendly terms with the chauffeur but it was impossible. When I was given Lenin's Prize I bought a refrigerator, and I remember the chauffeur's wife who was crying in the kitchen, saying, "There you go, some can allow themselves certain things and others can't."

It was very unpleasant to see these neighbors always stressed out and sullen because we were "getting rich."

It was in the bathroom that I wrote *Ballad of a Soldier*.

At the time, almost all directors lived in communal apartments. Naumov did not, because his father was a well-known cameraman: Naum Naumov-Strazh.[13] But Malov and Paradzhanov lived in kommunalki, as did many others.

In 1962, I shot *Clear Skies*, a film that also had aroused the censors' suspicions. It was Nikita Khrushchev again who saved it. Times were already very different, you could criticize bureaucrats.

But liberalization had its limit. An accountant for our group wrote a letter of complaint against me to the Central Committee, saying that I spat in our Party's face. It was a film that was too violently anti-Stalin and deStalinization was poorly regarded by the Party apparatus and by the people. And I had implicated the system.

The Minister of Culture at the time, Ekaterina Furtseva,[14] demanded to see the film immediately. She came herself to Mosfilm, with at least 20 colleagues. The film was not edited but she asked to see it none-the-less, showing me the accountant's letter of complaint.

So she watched the film with her colleagues, no music and no sound. At the end of the screening, she said, "yes, it is a movie" and everyone repeated "yes, it is a movie." Then after a minute of silence she added, "But this is all true."

"And then the girl is a good actor."

"Oh yes, she is a good actor," the choir of colleagues would repeat. It was very amusing.

When we got out of the screening room, she whispered to me: "Come in the elevator with me and press the button as soon as we are in so that nobody else enters." I obeyed, and she told me: "Your film is good, I'll give you money to finish it. I only ask that you delineate the difference between the two eras: Khrushchev's and Stalin's. The rest you can keep as is."

I edited shots of a thaw between the two periods.

It is thanks to Ekaterina Furtseva and to Khrushchev that I was finally able to leave my communal apartment. I was asked to shoot a film where a Russian pilot was the first to break the sound barrier. Having found out that it was not true and that the Americans had done it a year and a half before the Soviets, I refused to continue.

When one refuses a film, the employees, from the driver to the make-up artist do not receive their bonus. They get their salary no matter what but the bonus depends on actual shooting. So I took the project back but I improvised, and the result was totally different.

## 92 / Soviet Communal Living

We got called in to the Central Committee, who had "ordered" the film, and we were received by Mrs. Furtseva, who was also member of the CC. The director of Mosfilm was quaking in fear because we had improvised and that was completely prohibited. But I understood that everything was fine from the secretary's smile.

Mrs. Furtseva congratulated us and said, "The secretary general Nikita Khrushchev saw the film with the Politburo and he liked it. Congratulations. He asked me to pass on his regards and to enquire whether you need anything."

"Nothing thank you," I answered. But the studio's director then intervened: "What, didn't you know? Grigory Naumovich wrote *Ballad of a Soldier* in a bathroom, interrupted by a neighbour who made scenes because he occupied it too long."

That is how I received my own individual, three room apartment with a balcony.

CHAPTER 20

# Lenins, Nothing But Lenins

"And Fyodor Pavlovich ?"
"He went to get some screens and brick. They'll build partitions."
"Damned outrage!"
"They'll be moving additional tenants into all the apartments, Philip Philippovich, except yours."

—Mikhail Bulgakov. *Heart of a Dog*

I lived in a 16-square-meter room in a kommunalka on Chekhov Street in the center of Moscow, which was also my studio. There I painted thousands of Lenins, small, big, standard-sized ones, non-standard-sized ones. Not all are signed Boris Vitalievich Kalinovsky because not being a member of the Artist's Union, I often ghostpainted for other painters.

I was born in 1912. My father, Vitaly Kalinovsky, was a military man of aristocratic origin. He was in the army with Admiral Kolchak.[1] I always loved drawing from early childhood and never had to ask myself what I would do when I grew up.

A well-known linguist lived in this four-room apartment with us. Not having enough space in his room, he would give lessons to his students in the corridor. He was divorced, his ex-wife lived at the end of the corridor! In the fourth room lived a masseur, who worked for the sports club Moscow Dinamo.

This community lasted 25 years. I painted Lenins on command, the orders coming from a special fund that brought together all the "Lenin

94 / Soviet Communal Living

portrait painters" who would then take care of reselling the portraits they bought from us.

For an artist in the USSR, painting Lenin and Stalin was "easy street." We were sure to sell them, and it was well paid. Every "standard" portrait, small and only showing the face was priced at 350 rubles.[2] As for me, I was particularly good at big paintings, which paid from 5,000 to 7,000 rubles.

I was earning a lot of money. I was not really rich but I had a car, a Moskvich[3] that I had bought after the war for 9,000 rubles, and that I kept for 30 years. I gave myself this present, thanks to a portrait of Stalin that sold very well.

My output was eight to ten "standard" portraits of Lenin and a "non-standard" one each month. In any case, this was the "norm."[4] First I painted Lenin and Stalin, then Lenin and Khrushchev, then the whole Politburo. There were many of us painting "standard" portraits but big full-length decorated portraits, there were only two or three of us doing them in Moscow.

Of course I had never seen Lenin, I was way too insignificant, and then it never occurred to them. Stalin, I saw him only once, from afar. Really I can say that I never saw either of the two even though I spent my life painting them.

I painted from photographs. I have a few unpublished photographs of Lenin that came from the TASS agency's[5] secret archive and that were given to me as models.

Of course, each of us had "our own" Lenin. Mine sold well because I had "felt" his character straight away and always succeeded at the first brush stroke.

Each year, the Fund established a list of inspirational themes: "the Lenin-Stalin friendship," "the kolkhoz," etc. There would be six or seven composition themes, we only had to choose one and paint.

Painting Lenin was so prestigious that the question of another theme would not even arise. Controls were very strict. First the Artistic Council had to check.[6] The painting would then be submitted to the "expertise" of a group of party officials whose only job consisted of examining the portraits and making sure that there were no "deviations" in them, physical or ideological.

I am not a member of the Artists Union, and I have never belonged to the Party. I was afraid to lie and of being obliged to say that my father was aristocratic and that he had been part of Admiral Kolchak's troops. That is probably why I was never given a studio even though I was recognized as one of the best.

I stacked my "standard" Lenins and Stalins at my place in a corner of the room. The big canvases, which were two meters long or high, were always a problem. Therefore, one day I put a big Lenin in the corridor.

At night when the neighbors came back from work, I saw them hesitate, stop in front of the portrait and finally bow with respect. I was in my room and had left the door open and saw them all bow, one after the other. They had the same respectful, slightly scared reaction as one who enters a church. This shows how strong Lenin's cult was in this country.

As I was not a member of the Artists Union, I ghostpainted a lot, especially when Khrushchev forbade non-Union members to paint Lenin.

One day I decided to paint Stalin on Lenin's favorite bench. I painted a railing and a rural background behind him, the scene was supposed to take place in Gorky, the city where Lenin had stayed when he was ill. The portrait was discussed for two years.

Sysoev[7] had decided that I deserved to compete for the Stalin Prize, at the time a major award for an artist. It was 1951, two years before Stalin's death, a photo of my piece had been passed on to Anastas Mikoyan.[8] We never received an answer.

At the Academy of Art, they got frightened by such an audacious painting. Alexander Gerasimov, president of the Academy, was against it, but all the other members voted for me. One round, second round, third round. In theory that was it, I had won.

But Gerasimov decided a fourth round would be organized, exceptionally so. In the meantime, in my absence, they had started criticizing it saying there was too little luminosity on Stalin and so forth and so on. And when the fourth scrutiny was finally held, all but four voted against it. I was in the room next door, shaking hands and being congratulated. I owe my white hair to this story, for two years I was worried stiff, this piece was the peak of my artistic career...

The Fund still bought it for 75,000 roubles. My Stalin left for Sverdlovsk,[9] and I never knew anything about it anymore.

CHAPTER 21

# Dissidence

> The general meeting asks you voluntarily and by way of labor discipline to give up your dining room. Nobody has a dining room in Moscow.
> "Not even Isadora Duncan", the woman cried in a ringing voice.
> [...] "Uhum," said Philip Philippovich in a strange voice. "And where am I to take my meals?"
> "In the bedroom", the four answered in chorus.
> —Mikhail Bulgakov, *Heart of a Dog*

My father cannot truly be classified as a dissident even though it is through him and Andrey Siniavsky that the dissident movement began in the USSR. First and foremost, he was a clandestine man of letters.

When he was arrested by the KGB in 1965, dissidence as such did not yet exist. When he was liberated in 1970, it was already an organized movement.

In the '50s when I was a child, we lived in a very old house not far from the Polytechnic Museum, which is today the Byelorussian embassy. Dating from the eighteenth century, the building had belonged to a noble of Catherine II's court. It is an architectural monument.

We lived on the fourth floor in a very large apartment of eight or nine rooms, originally used by the servants. The rooms were strangely designed. Walls had been erected to make it a kommunalka, rooms were not really square but corners and angles.

We had two rooms in this apartment. One of the two was long and skinny like half of a herring. It was very dark there. Yuly Daniel, my father, worked in the tiny crookedly shaped one.

Because he liked to write lying down, he had bought a couch but it did not fit in the room. For a long time, he studied all of the possible ways of sawing it, but he made a mistake on one side and once the couch was installed in the room my father had his nose to the wall.

One entered via the kitchen where there were five or six stoves and a sink. It was a very old kitchen, slightly raised, black with soot, and with a beamed ceiling from which emerged huge rusty nails. When I was little, my mother would tell me that undoubtedly it was an old torture chamber.

The inhabitants of the apartment were truly international on an ethnic, social, and historical level.

We, we were a family of Jewish intellectuals. My mother was a teacher, a linguist, my father, he had stopped teaching around 1954 and had become a poetry translator. My mother was not a Muscovite, she came from Kharkov.

Both of them had to leave Moscow for some time at the end of the '40s, during the antisemitic campaign. They settled in Kaluga[1] where they were teachers. They came back in 1954–1955 and found these two rooms.

A Jewish family also lived in the room next to ours. They were very refined people, very conscious of their Jewishness. Eshil Israelevich Maisel was a Jewish bibliography expert, and his wife Felicia Lazirievna was a high-level interpreter. They had a daughter, Ella, and a maid who slept in the corridor behind a curtain, Marusia. The maid had come from the country, and undoubtedly was a cleaning lady in order to have a bed in Moscow.

We were very good friends, the Maisels had antique furniture and seemed rich to me, even if they were as poor as us.

The next room was occupied by a single woman, an engineer. My parents told me that she'd been married to a KGB agent, whom she had divorced.

Then arrived a wonderful Tatar family, the Ibrahimovs. They were five of them: Diadia Volodia, Tiotia Sonia, and their three children. They always received parents of parents, friends of friends, like us. They also had two rooms in a row, they were very poor but joyful, they shouted all the time but with lightheartedness. Diadia Volodia was a porter at the Kazan station, like many Tatars.

Sonia was actually called Setkhan, the others also had Tatar names but we had renamed them to make it easier.

Once a year, their parents came from the Tatar countryside to visit them for a Muslim celebration, perhaps it was Kuram Bairam. Prior to the celebration they would collect money, one of them went to Kasimov, a Tatar city in the Riazan area, and would buy a horse. They would cut its throat and prepare a special dish with horse meat, which they would feast on.

Every year, they would ask to borrow our room for a day or two for this celebration. The mullah would come to the house and bless it. I was very amused by it all of course.

The corridor then made a semicircle, and in the last big room lived Natalia Dmitrievna V., a high aristocrat who had finished Smolny Institute in St. Petersburg. This woman was a real remnant of the Empire, a real "smolianka" with aristocratic manners. She was the daughter of a cavalry colonel and had spent vacations in the barracks when she was a child, she had a stiffness and distinctiveness that was very military.

In the kitchen when the Tatars would swear, she would intervene with her inimitable French accent and tell them: "Sonia, you must not speak that way, it is not correct." She wore an embroidered bathrobe, lived alone with her daughter Natasha, and worked in a microbiology institute.

The kitchen in the morning would fill up with all these people: the Jew would arrive with his incunabulums, his wife pronouncing sentences in the last language she was studying, the Tatar would swear in Tatar and the aristocrat corrected everybody.

I do not remember any dramas. Tamara and I were the youngest, we were very spoiled, especially Tamara who was very pretty. I could go freely between all the rooms, except for the aristocrat's where I would have to knock. I loved visiting it because the room was filled with objects, statues, and knick-knacks, which attracted me.

We did not have hot water, there was no bathroom, and water had to be heated.

We left in 1959. We were thrown out of this lodging at the time of "Khrushchoby."[2] The Tatars had gotten a separate apartment but we, we were not as lucky. We were sent to Leninsky Prospect, the last Moscow houses before the countryside. It was a huge compound of 16 entrances and 10 floors that had just finished being built.

We had two rooms there: 24 square meters in total with hot water, toilets, and a bathroom. The apartment was made up of three rooms: in the third one, 14 square meters, lived a Red Proletariat factory worker with his mother, who was 90 years old.

So there were much fewer of us but a small kommunalka is worse than a big one: first because the toilets were often in the bathroom and second because there is no real corridor.

A whole section of the building in front of ours was reserved for Central Commitee officials, I would see Pobedas[3] parked at the entrances. For me those people were the rich. So my astonishment was enormous when I was invited to visit a classmate, Seriozha, the son of Vladimir Kriuchkov[4] for the first time. Their apartment did not give the impression of wealth. At the time, Kriuchkov was a Party civil servant, who had returned from Hungary where he'd worked at the embassy. There was not a single book at their place, that is why I had the impression they were poor.

Our neighbors were dedicated communists. One day, I heard the old mother say: "I had a vision of Nadezhda Konstantinovna Krupskaia, my time has probably come."[5] However, they were honest, very tolerant, being our neighbor was definitely not easy.

We did not have a good sense of orderliness, and our door was always open and we always had guests, some stayed overnight. Pavel Ilyich, the communist neighbor, contented himself with making faces but he didn't say anything, never protested.

When the KGB started suspecting my father's clandestine activities, they installed microphones in the apartment, and Pavel Ilyich's participation was necessary. My mother and he never spoke to each other after my father was arrested. One day my mother said to him, "You know my husband was arrested." And he answered, "I did notice that he had not been around the house for a long time." That was all.

However, before his death at the hospital where he was being treated for cancer, he asked one of his parents to call my mother to his bedside. "Do you remember Larisa when I took in my nephew in 1965?"

"Yes," she said.

"Well, it was not my nephew Larisa, it was not my nephew," he let out breathlessly. He did not want to die with that burden on his conscience.

He was not mean, and he did not do it on his own initiative but when the KGB asked him to take in a workman to place the microphones, he had not been able to refuse.

He died in 1968.

In August 1968, my mother was arrested.[6] She had become a "dissident," in the real sense of the term, an avowed opponent of the regime, after the Siniavsky-Daniel trial in February 1966 and my father's arrest. Our apartment was on the ground floor, it was easy to observe her from the windows.

In 1969, a family settled into the old communist's room. I was living alone then; I was 20 years old, my two parents in prison. I got on exceptionally badly with these people, a young couple, biologists with a child. We argued constantly.

When my mother came back from her exile in eastern Siberia, in 1971, her neighbor in this apartment was a "limitchik" from Mariupol in Ukraine. This young girl was very compassionate of my mother's fate as a dissident but of course, here as well the KGB intervened. Natasha herself, told us how she had been called in and interrogated.

Today, I have definitive evidence that Natasha did talk, but she did not say all that she knew. In fact she got the room on condition that she spy on the inhabitants so she knew what she had to do.

She was probably told that CIA agents lived there. But when she saw we were normal people who did not feed on human flesh, she changed her attitude toward us.

After his liberation in 1970, my father was separated from my mother and was authorized to live in Kaluga, once again in a communal apartment. His neighbors seemed to have come out straight out of a B-movie: a very, very beautiful young couple, tall and blond, waiters at the hotel-restaurant Intourist-Kaluga. They were obviously KGB, like all waiters in hard currency hotels. My father had abandoned his clandestine activities at the time, but he was still a celebrity and his visitors, his phone calls etc., were all very closely watched.

As for me, I had been living in an individual apartment from 1973, the year of my first marriage, to 1977 the year of my first divorce. In the USSR, the twists and turns of communal and noncommunal life are very often linked to numerous divorces and encounters.

I was closely watched by the police at that time and had to be careful. I worked as a program engineer. I tried moving back to the apartment on Lenin Perspective but the police told me "Nyet": "You may not because they are two communicating rooms and you are not the same sex as your mother…"[7]

My second wife was not from Moscow, she was not registered anywhere, we were very happy when the police finally agreed to register us in a building in Medvedkovo,[8] miles from anywhere. What's more, I am still registered there; I live "clandestinely" in this centrally located kommunalka with my last wife who is registered there.

In Medvedkovo, we had 12 square meters in three rooms. The retiree who lived there with his wife denounced me, today I have the proof of it. He did not really hide it anyway, he'd come into the kitchen and tell me, "So Sasha, what are you doing these days?" "Hey Sasha, are you going to do that samizdat or not, you'll give me a pamphlet, won't you?" I lied to him, "Leave me alone, you are provoking me, I do not do things like that."

But my room did not have a lock anymore, and he would go in it when we were out. We would find papers rifled. Of course, we wouldn't do anything serious at home, we never spoke of our clandestine activities. We would telephone from the street, done not only in communal apartments by the way, calling from the street was common under Brezhnev.

At home we would write on little scraps of paper, a classic situation in the '70s. Some foreign friends gave us a present of "magic paper"[9] an essential accessory in a dissident's living room. The KGB knew about it, moreover they were constantly taking away our "stiralki"[10] during the searches, which they'd confiscate just to enrage us.

An old lady, part of whose family had been shot under Stalin, would often come to see my mother when my father was in the Gulag. One day, she made a gesture with her hand asking for pencil and paper. She wrote: "So, did you have the meeting?"

"No," answered my mother aloud.

Then the old lady wrote, "What bastards."

CHAPTER 22

# The Passageway Room

I lived in a communal apartment, in a huge building put up before the
Revolution by the "Russia" Insurance Company for its employees. The
apartment had been planned for one family, but now four were living
in it.

—Andrei Amalrik. *Involuntary Journey to Siberia*

I lived 30 years in Baku,[1] in a passageway room. Do you know what passageway rooms are? They are rooms that all the inhabitants pass through, simple partitions separate you from your neighbors. At our place, a corridor was made at the end of the room, but we were not authorized to put up the partition, which was wooden, all the way to the ceiling. The room was very high, 4 meters, and the firemen didn't want it because of safety reasons, or so they said.

This communal apartment belonged at one time to my grandfather who was an industrial candymaker.

So the neighbors, a mother and her daughter, could literally hear everything that happened in our room, where I lived with my mother and my father. They were Jewish like us but from a much less well-off background than ours. The daughter who was in her 40s was a dressmaker, she made men's shirts. My whole childhood was punctuated by the rhythm of the sound of her sewing machine. The old lady who passed through our room suffered from all sorts of illnesses. But above all she had arthritis of the knees for which she used a salve that was so pungent that the smell is still with me. I smelt her when she crossed the corridor, the fragrance of Soviet salves were rarely delicate.

I was raised with the permanent "ssshhh" of my parents, it was a complete obsession; in fact, later, after moving to a kommunalka in Moscow, I raised my son in the same way. And yet the house in Baku was not a kingdom of silence. Azerbaijan, Russian, and Armenian families of different traditions and religions coexisted in the apartments. Arguments or simple stresses were never-ending. My mother didn't know how to cook. When she was little she had a cook who forbade her to come into the kitchen. Ah well, the neighbors never invited us to share their holiday cakes.

The windows were always open, it's hot on the Caspian Sea, and our building looked out on a large round courtyard, which resembled a well. We would regularly hear a woman fling herself at the window and yell, "They put petroleum in my casserole, they put petroleum in my casserole." So everyone would rush to the window and out would pour her commentary.

Putting petroleum in casseroles was the equivalent of the famous Moscow spit. A common fear in the kommunalka was that one of the neighbors had spat in the casserole, one has to say that certain apartments harbored people who were fully capable of such an act. There were even casseroles that existed with a special closure that you screwed on to prevent your neighbor from lifting the lid.

In 1968 we "went up" to Moscow with my husband who was a researcher, and we found a room in a communal apartment on Kirov Street, opposite the old post office, which is today the Stock Exchange. The building had belonged to the grandfather of Nikita Mikhalkov, the director.[2]

Four families shared this apartment which was very difficult to live in because it did not have a corridor. All the rooms came off of a little square entryway, a sort of patio.

We had a room of 13 square meters. I mention it because if we had had 15 square meters, we would never have gotten the second room that we were allocated in the same apartment after my son's birth.[3]

In order to move to Moscow we had given a large sum of money to a Muscovite who had agreed to exchange her room for ours in Baku, a strictly illegal operation—exchanges were only authorized within the boundaries of the same city and between people regularly registered with the police.

The Passageway Room / 105

One of our neighbors was a jeweler and made jewelry at night. This was illegal. She could have been guilty of speculation, of working at home, and God knows what other abomination. But nobody denounced her, we would hear her working secretly every night. Her family was comprised of four people, all adults, in 13 square meters. The grandfather had tuberculosis; he committed suicide by throwing himself out of the window of their room. The grandmother was not much better, she was very irritable and was constantly making remarks to us; she put an end to herself by throwing herself under a tram.

Another neighbor got up at 5:30 to go to the factory. She was always afraid of being late because she worked in a numbered factory,[4] under strict control. If she were late by one minute, it would cause her a lot of problems.[5] She prevented us from sleeping and caused the floorboards to vibrate with her high heels, but she was so nice that we never complained. But one day we gave her a present of some slippers.

We would wait for her to leave, go back to sleep, and the second neighbor would wake up at 6:30. We would wait for them to leave and then we would get up.

I often have a dream where we'd change apartments. They give us a beautiful apartment, filled with light, in a nice city. I visit all the rooms, one after another, I cry out in admiration, I'm happy when all of a sudden a door that I did not notice appears on the wall, it opens and a neighbor appears out of nowhere. I realize with terror that it is a communal apartment, and I wake up in a sweat.

I've had this dream for years, the apartments are different, the neighbors are different, but the nightmare is always the same.

CHAPTER 23

# The Prostitute

"Perhaps Isadora Duncan dines in her office and dissects rabbits in the bathroom. But I am not Isadora Duncan !..." he barked suddenly, and the purple of his face turned yellow.

"I shall dine in the dining room, and operate in the surgery!"

—Mikhail Bulgakov. *Heart of a Dog*

After the Parasite Law,[1] Vera I. remarked to me in a caustic tone of voice, "Vera P., I never see your husband go off to work." With good reason, he was a painter and worked in the rooms that we occupied in the apartment. But when he answered that he was preparing sketches for Poster Publications—a political publisher—she got scared and despite her jealousy, didn't dare interfere.

Vera I. worked for the KGB. She was drunk from morning to night and lived in a small accommodation where the owner of this beautiful building on the Arbat had previously lived. When I was little I met him once with my mother, he was wearing a fur coat as men often did before the Revolution.

I've been living here since I was four years old; I've never known anything other than this six room communal accommodation. I'm 60 today, my grandparents, the V.s rented this apartment, which became a collective in the '20s. But we could only keep two rooms.

My grandmother who was the principal of a school and a big disciple of Nadezhda Krupskaia, Lenin's wife, was an activist of coeducational and atheistic education. But her family, that was of aristocratic origin, continued to observe religious customs.

My grandmother was on good terms with the administration of the building, that's doubtless why we enjoyed privileged conditions for a long time, but she undoubtedly bribed Vera I. Moreover, as soon as my grandmother died, Vera changed her attitude toward us, and that was when she raised the question of my husband's work.

After the war, the house was very joyful even if there were a lot of us, 13 in all. My best friend lived in the next room and communal life seemed easy to me. My friend shared her room with her divorced mother and her little brother and came to visit our luxurious two rooms, she mainly loved our antique furniture and the few dishes we had left. I had the sensation of being much richer, I even had a guilt complex.

In the '60s, the mentality changed. Immediately after the war, nobody balked when it was their turn to wash the floor. But when people started getting individual accommodations, their psychology changed. The renters were no longer concerned with maintaining the kommunalka because there was the desire to leave. Even though there hadn't been any before, this was when the cockroaches[2] showed up.

In 1969, two old people arrived in the next room, the G.s. He was an old sailor, a real Russian man, he had been in all the wars, the Revolution, the civil war, the Finnish war,[3] and World War II. One of those men, who you can still encounter today in the alleys of Gorky Park during the Revolution's anniversary, when old soldiers with their jackets covered with clinking medals, reunite.

They lived under miserable conditions feeding themselves on pickles and vodka. We had good relations even if during the night the husband would go out in the corridor forgetting that he was not in the country. His wife was fat and sick, so we had to do the housework for them.

Then they got it into their heads that one of our neighbors, Volodia V., wanted to poison them. V. was a real parasite, one of the alcoholics of Khrushchev's generation, who took advantage of the system without doing anything. It's true that he pestered them, the old G. woman was supposed to collect the money for the electricity and Volodia didn't want to pay, he didn't stop annoying her.

He did it to everybody by the way. Whenever we were coming back after midnight, we'd leave a message "Please do not shut the door." But V. would do whatever he wished, and I always had to get up to open the door for him. He'd come back alone, drunk, and immediately start beating his wife.

Anyway, the old G. woman was sure that he had made a hole in the wall and was poisoning them little by little by blowing gas into their room. She had never seen this hole, it was a preconceived idea, paranoia is typical in a communal apartment. She lodged a complaint, convened an inquiry committee, and called us as witnesses.

But when the committee came, I wasn't able to lie about the gas affair, and the old people took it very badly. They got mad, begged to be given another room and left.

In 1979 G. Sh. arrived. She appeared one fine day with a man, pretending this room had been awarded to her. She didn't have any papers but I believed her, otherwise how could she have known that a room was free? She tearfully told me that she needed help, that she had been abandoned.

In fact she had a child, a newborn who cried all the time. She was an alcoholic. This is how I found myself spending my days washing a newborn's diapers, whom she left all alone, not even bothering to feed it. My daughter-in-law went to the police to complain about nonassistance but it took a year and a half before they finally took him away from her.

G. brought men to the house, she needed money to drink. She was a Tatar, had a vulgar beauty. Everyone gave way when she cried, which she could do at the slightest whim—in addition, she was remarkably eloquent for someone who had no schooling.

She was 18 years old. The comings-and-goings began only a few days after her arrival. She'd come to the house alone, go to her room, five minutes later the bell would ring, she'd go open the door and say that she had neighbors and not to make any noise. Then sounds of battle would come from her room because apparently she did not want to succumb to these men's advances. She'd come out running and would flee out the service door of the apartment.

Inevitably the men would come knock at our door because she'd always steal their wallets! She only brought rich ones home, those who had a car.

She had a second baby who was born alcoholic; he was always needy and cried day and night. I called a doctor who had them remove the child.

We then convened the police to let them know that we had a prostitute in the house. The police didn't want to know anything, "In our country, prostitution does not exist."[4]

One day she stole my daughter-in-law's bag, the police told us, "It's your business, we don't concern ourselves with the goings-on inside the apartment." We didn't dare take it any further, this was during Brezhnev's time, and everyone was afraid.

When she went to restaurants with her men, upon leaving the place she would put on the "shapkas" (hats) and coats of other clients. It made us laugh, we always saw her with new clothes.

She was finally arrested after having robbed an apartment. But her aunt who was a saleswoman in the store "Okean"[5] and had the savoir-faire; she immediately offered us fish that was impossible to find other than on the black market at a decent price. It was to buy our silence, she wanted her niece to be judged as a simpleton, and she succeeded. We heard them sniggering on the telephone about this.

G. left the house after being judged mentally ill, and her madness got her an individual apartment. In the USSR sane people had to squeeze 15 into 3 rooms but the crazies had to live alone, it was provided for by law...In addition, they gave her three rooms because she had two children, which made everybody laugh.

Today my daughter-in-law and my grandson live in the prostitute's old room, we managed to get it last year. My son left his wife and lives elsewhere but he comes back often, first to see us, my husband and me, and also because his painting studio is here. All this does not make relations any easier....

CHAPTER 24

# The French Lover

> There was one bell for all the tenants. If the caller was for us he rang
> five times.
>
> —Andrei Amalrik. *Involuntary Journey to Siberia*

I'm a Russian from Kazakhstan. I was born in a small village in the South,
I studied there, in Alma Ata,[1] but I always wanted to live in Moscow. In
August 1970, Vladimir Vysotsky[2] came on tour to Kazakhstan, I was 20
years old then, I was very bold, I went to see him at the hotel, and I made
his acquaintance.

I brought him to my father who loved his songs; we lived in a little
house with a garden. He played his guitar and sang, my father recorded
him for five hours, and he stayed until five in the morning.

The next morning my father was called into the KGB, they told him,
"You received the anti-Soviet Visotsky in your home, and you recorded
him, give us the cassette." My father figured it out and gave them a different cassette.

I saw Volodia when he came back to Alma Ata with the Taganka
Theater Company. I spoke to him about my wish to live in Moscow; he
introduced me to some friends who helped me. The only possibility was
a sham marriage[3] so I married a man who was 12 years older than me
and who disappeared after pocketing the money. I installed myself in the
room where he was registered, which he didn't need because he lived at his
mother's. But when we decided to divorce so that I could officially register

in that room, the authorities announced that this was undoubtedly a "false divorce" (!!) and that we had only to hang a curtain to divide our room, which was quite large—25 square meters—in two.

I lived for two years by myself; the second room in the apartment was unoccupied. Then in 1976 a couple moved in. A few months later they had a little girl who is my goddaughter.

At the time I worked at Mosfilm. That was the year that I met J.-C., he was French, the representative of a French medical equipment business that had a contract with the hospital of the Ministry of the Interior. He was in Moscow at least six months of the year, if not more. I loved him as I've never loved anyone and as I'll never love anyone again. That love emptied me.

We lived at my place, in my kommunalka, he found some sort of crazy exoticism in this. Here was my neighbor's baby, its two grandmothers, its parents... he was obliged to wash in the kitchen, we didn't have a bathroom, the neighbors came in and out and he'd say to me, "You know where I come from only the king washes like this, among all these people." Our neighbors were very affectionate with us. They never denounced him. He was a little scared, in fact, at my work a colleague who spotted him when he came to pick me up, said that I was with the KGB. "All the time that she's been with that Frenchman, and nobody bothers her, it's rather fishy," she said to another colleague who was a friend of mine.

He always kept his hotel room but most of the time he was at my place. We even went on a trip together, he came to Alma Ata to my parents who were very fond of him, even though they knew he was married. We lived an unbelievable passion for seven years.

In 1978 Maxim Shoshtakovich, the son of the musician, told me that I was crazy to act this way, and that it would end badly. We were at a hotel in Pitsunda on the Black Sea, we had taken two rooms, but he spent all night in my room, it was very dangerous, these hotels were closely watched by the women on each floor, hotel personnel inevitably worked for the secret service....

My goddaughter, little Julia, adored him, she still has a doll named after him. His friends all came to the house, he knew all my neighbors who were of a completely different background, but adorable, we ate and drank all together.

He was the most jealous man I've ever met, he thought that I'd had an affair with Vissotsky which is not true. We saw each other regularly at Mosfilm but didn't spend much time together.

In 1980, when Visotsky died, J.-C. was not in Moscow. Volodia died on July 25 and on the 28th I went to the Taganka Theater where you could pay your last respects. I've never seen such a crowd. I stopped on the way to buy some flowers and the saleswoman said to me, "It's for Vissotsky, right?" There wasn't even one line in the newspaper, not a word on the radio but Taganka Place was black with people. The Olympics had already started.

I was scared to take my camera, I've always regretted it. The sun shone brilliantly, the area was taken over by militia on horseback. I remember a man who undoubtedly had come out of the hospital to attend the funeral; he had a white bandage on his forehead spotted with red. Nikita Mikhalkov was there, and then an astronaut whose name I've forgotten, undoubtedly people began to be less afraid, to brave the authorities. When I returned home the neighbor told me that J.-C. had telephoned numerous times—he wanted to know where I'd been.

Our affair continued another three years. Then in 1983, J.-C. started coming less often to Moscow, I think he'd met another woman. One day he called me to tell me that it was over, that he was sorry, that he asked my forgiveness. "Thank you for everything, forgive me," he said.

I don't know how I survived. For me, every stone in the city, every square centimeter in this apartment was linked to this Frenchman. For seven years I had lived only for him, by him, in the morning I would get up before him, I'd jump in a taxi and go the kolkhoz market to buy him some strawberries so that he'd have them when he woke up. I think I loved him the way you love a child.

After his abandonment, my neighbors in the apartment helped me enormously, not to let me die. I did nothing but smoke and drink coffee, I no longer fed myself. I sold everything that was Western at my place, the record player, some clothes, I thought I was going crazy for four years.

My neighbors left on November 6, 1985; they'd been given an individual apartment. I liked calling them, I was so used to living with them, I cried as if someone had died. They left me the keys to their room, which was not legal.

There were some attempts to install people here but it didn't happen, I don't have a bathroom, it's too small and the room to be occupied overlooks the exchanger, it's too noisy.

In 1986, I started working in an art gallery, and then I felt better but this love is always in my head, he took my best years, from 26 to 33.

When I have a little time I'm going to take on privatizing my apartment, but it's almost impossible. I have to privatize my room, and via a lawyer friend I can automatically add the next room, which has been recognized as being unfit for habitation due to the noise. But everything is very complicated, normally I wouldn't even have the right to my 25 meters. I had to make myself a fake certificate saying that I am a reputable painter. Thanks to this paper I have the right to an extra 10 square meters. I'm doing all this because I have to do something.

CHAPTER 25

# Masha L. and the Spirit of the Kommunalka

> My wife, you know, was young and good natured. She didn't have a room.
> I thought that on account of this bathroom she'd refuse me, and I did not foresee any family happiness and comfort, but she didn't refuse at all.
> —Mikhaïl Zoshchenko. *Scenes from the Bathhouse*

I was born in Perm, in the Urals in 1960. We lived in the center of town on Young Communist Avenue, in a three-room communal apartment, occupied by three families.

Tiotia Ania, one of the inhabitants, looked after us once in a while, the daughter of the "neighbors" and me, to allow our parents to go out. I remember her, she was very nice but an alcoholic. Sometimes mother would say that she didn't want to leave me with her, I didn't understand why until later.

Then my mother got divorced, and we left Perm for Kharkov in Ukraine where we had family. There too we lived in a communal apartment, but secretly—we didn't have a "propiska." We shared an 11-square-meter room with my great-grandmother, two of her granddaughters one of whom was my mother, and me. We lived almost a full year all together, nothing but women.

In the other room lived street entertainers, a rather elderly couple with two dogs. They were dog trainers. The kitchen, tiny, had only one stove. There were toilets, no bathroom, and no hot water. It was around 1965 in a big house in the center of the city.

We ate very well, I mainly remember strawberries and tomatoes. The apartment was very decrepit, the narrow room with the high ceiling made me think of a coffin.

And then we left for Moscow, where mother was registered before her marriage. This was in 1969. We installed ourselves with the ex-wife of my mother's father who had remarried with a certain Nikolai. They lived on the ground floor on a little street near the Kursk train station.

Mother had written a letter to Kosygin[1] asking him to "return" the propiska that she had lost upon leaving for Perm. She got it a year and a half later, and she found work for 90 rubles a month.

Four families shared four rooms. We all slept in the same room, even the big German shepherd had his place in a corner. The beds were infested with bugs that made dozens of little red bite marks. They asked me what they were in school, I was too embarrassed to answer. I was already eight years old.

The room next to ours was occupied by a very elderly couple, Barbara and her blind husband.

Further down the corridor lived a KGB man and his family. Everybody knew that he worked for the intelligence services. They often left on trips and for quite long periods, I remember that they went to Chad and to Venezuela. I didn't know anything about these countries, other than that they were hot. In Moscow they had their car, a Volga, it was a big luxury at the time, and they replaced it fairly often. They even had a foreign car, extremely rare, and the wife had various clothes made of the same color as the vehicle, which fascinated me. For me it was the epitomy of snobbism. She was young and beautiful and wore wigs, it was very fashionable in the end of the '60s. She was named Nina like my mother.

It wasn't long after that I learned that the husband was KGB. At the time of our cohabitation, I was too young to understand. He was chubby, very nice, offered us candy, his children had very different toys from my own. This was not a time of food shortages but his children had chewing gum, which didn't exist in the USSR, and I only dreamed of this.

The last couple that lived in our apartment did not come often; they had an individual accommodation in the Moscow area and only kept a little room in this kommunalka for convenience.

The kitchen window looked out on a courtyard where a space for the dogs had been set up. While preparing meals one had huge mounds of dog excrement under one's eyes, it was disgusting and practical at the same time because our Mishka went for a walk there himself.

I lived in this apartment from the age of 5 to 12. I have nagging memories of dust, of the smell of dust, visions of dusty furniture. I sometimes went to a friend who lived in an individual two rooms with her parents, for me it was a dream, even if the buildings, the famous "Khrushchoby" were in a lamentable state. Their apartment had a bathroom with a toilet, with an impregnable view of the neighborhood's garbage but that was not important. For me, it was luxury, the impossible dream.

The idea of a bathroom has a major importance for me. In Perm and in Kharkov we didn't have one. When I was little, mother washed me in a big iron tub, those tubs that are also used to wash laundry and that you still see hanging on the bathroom walls of kommunalki.

Then we lived in an apartment with a bathroom, and mother washed me very thoroughly once a week. People who are in their 60s today have kept this habit of washing only once a week, many for a long time only knew "Russian Baths," public bathing establishments.

Since the age of seven, I'd been in a special Russian-French school where I did all my studies. The two children of the KGB agent also studied in the same school, which was in the next courtyard.

At night, we ate dinner in our room, which acted as a living room as well as a dining room. Nobody eats in the kitchen in a communal apartment; it's a communal area always filled with lots of people but mainly an area that's too dirty to eat in, it's almost too dirty to cook in...

Our room was filled with rolls of paper and leather, my grandfather made flowers out of paper, shoes, and painted slippers for us. We were very squashed in our sleeping arrangements. Until I was 12, I always shared a bed with my mother.

All the doors in the apartment shut with a key but everyone knew where to find the keys in a communal armoire in the corridor. One day, mother was robbed, one of the inhabitants stole a French perfume from her, and a 100 rubles, at the time it was not an insignificant sum.

We did not have a television, but the couple who moved in once the blind man left had one. Sometimes in the evening, I went next door to the "neighbor's" room to watch television but my grandfather was very strict and rarely gave me permission. The neighbors, you always called them that, not even by their first name. "Neighbor, do you have some bread?" When you live in the same apartment, it's strange however, it makes for strange relationships!

When grandfather forbade me to watch television, I'd listen through the wall. At the time my mother was studying to be a railroad engineer. My grandfather, he was 60 years old and often played checkers by himself in the room.

Then mother was hired by the Ministry of Railroads, a ministry that Stalin adored, and our life improved. We were awarded a room in a huge 200-square-meter apartment in the Three Station[2] area.

When we went to visit the apartment, I saw a little boy who was bicycling in the corridor, and I also announced that it was perfect. It was in 1972, mother was 32 years old and for the first time in her life she had a room all to herself. Well, obviously it was in a communal apartment, we still slept the two of us together, but we were no longer four or five.

It was a huge apartment originally with six rooms, with a 53-square-meter room divided in three, so there were a total of nine rooms.

In the first room Vera Nikolaevna, a French professor of around 50, lived alone. Then there was a small 18-square-meter room where a couple lived, he was in the military, she was an engineer, with a seven-year-old child and the wife's mother.

One of the children in the apartment was handicapped, he had an atrophied arm. He'd put on a prosthetic to go to school, as soon as he'd get home he'd take it off; on top of that his mother insisted he wear short-sleeved shirts, it was awful.

One day I was in the bathroom and I felt someone looking at me. He was perched on a kitchen chair and was looking at me through the high windows that separated the two rooms. I felt terribly bad, I was nauseous, and in the evening I complained to his mother. This story aggravated the latent feud between our families, we did not speak to each other for a very long time. In communal apartments, longish feuds were frequent. The handicapped boy was very intelligent but unbearable.

Then mother remarried a fantastic man, the three of us lived in this room, it was a little embarrassing for me, I was already 15. But luckily, a room in the apartment became free, and we were able to get it thanks to the minister.

The two rooms were separated by a long corridor. A new era began for me, I had the impression of living by myself. I threw out the furniture that I didn't like and only took books. I ate with my mother and my stepfather, I went to watch television at their place, that is at the other end of the corridor. This is what a kommunalka is, people who don't know it can't understand it.

It's in this house that I got married at the age of 24. The apartment was at 26 Krasnoprudnaya Street. The building had been built during Stalin's time for railroad workers. As it was close to the "Three Stations" you'd always meet strange people in the courtyard, drunk, who'd urinate everywhere. In Russia, all girls by the time they were 10 had had exhibitionist experiences. But in our courtyard their numbers were particularly high.

My feeling of freedom quickly disappeared. Mother had taken it very poorly to have someone else living at the house with me. And our coupledom was destroyed by a lack of intimacy, not even counting the curious neighbors who aggravated already existing tensions within our family.

After a year we decided to no longer eat our meals with her, to no longer shop with her, to try and save what remained to be saved, that is not too much. It had become unbearable, on top of which at the time she'd just lost her husband who had died.

You can imagine two young married people constantly constrained by the presence of other people, one of whom was a mother-in-law, old folks who were complete strangers to their families, hysterical women, and unbearable kids. For my husband who came from Ukraine and had never lived in a communal apartment, it was a rude shock. The marriage lasted two and a half years and was punctuated by very violent scenes between mother and me.

We ended up by divorcing. Mother was sure that the neighbors were a more successful couple than us, and overwhelmed me with reproaches. This young woman was a teacher, he was a chauffeur, they had two children, and my mother did not stop making tacit comparisons.

It was awful. Moreover I had a vision of an "idyllic couple" that was completely different. I knew for example that Natasha the teacher had not wanted her second child at all, she'd only had it to get the extra square meters, thus an independent apartment. I don't really admire calculating people...

Despite all her rights, and the unwanted child, Natasha had to wait 15 years anyway to get a new apartment. In Russia you don't wait for months or years but decades.

In a communal apartment, lack of privacy always ends up by people saying things they shouldn't. When her husband was named to East Germany and she knew that she was leaving with him, the wife of the KGB agent was so proud after long weeks of silence that she told me, "You know he's going to work in the secret service."

Discretion is impossible in a kommunalka. Every night watching more-or-less old casseroles in the kitchen and recognizing different food smells, you learn an enormous amount of details about the other inhabitants' lives. Same goes for the bathroom where this one or that one's lingerie is drying, as for the toilets...

I recognize the inhabitants of a communal apartment. The kommunalka leaves one more indifferent to whoever's next to you but also more suspicious and more aggressive. One speaks of "The Spirit of the Kommunalka" and the "Corridor System" with those doors that open and close or which are ajar for spying, those women who meet in the kitchen to gossip and discuss other people's daily lives. The smallest detail sometimes provokes the most endless quarrels that are an integral part of this sort of an apartment.

At our place, it was different, it was more the silence that was brutally imposed, no one talked to anyone else. The "Spirit of the Kommunalka" was the constant sensation of imminent danger. Some became more secretive, more timid, others on the contrary more cynical.

I recognize them in waiting lines, the inhabitants of communal apartments. They talk easily, shout louder than the others, you can see that they have the habit of analyzing the themes of daily life at length.

Everyone reacts differently to life in this type of apartment. It depends which period of life one's in and one's age, one's attitude changes.

But every apartment has its crazy person, just like every apartment has its drunk, its troublemakers, its informers, male or female, etc. For the crazies, it's mainly persecution manias; one neighbor convinced herself, for example, that the others were putting bits of glass in her bit of soap, or that they wanted to poison her. These obsessions can take on fantastic proportions, even leading to a lawsuit.

In one of my "lodgings" lived a little boy, about eight years old. He'd put the remains of a meal in corners of the corridor because he needed "to feed the animals." All of a sudden the apartment was filled with mice. But nobody could do anything because all the decisions that concerned the communal whole had to be unanimous and obviously the kid's parents voted against it....

My second husband had never lived in a communal apartment. When he enters the kitchen if someone is already there, he can't ignore them or turn his back on them. I can act like there's no one there. Whenever I have friends visit who live in communal apartments, I can see the difference. Those who live alone are very attentive when someone appears and very curious, whereas those who live in a kommunalka pay no attention or try and make a special impression on the newcomer by saying something strange in a very high voice.

The kommunalka involves a whole strategy of behavior. And when a conflict breaks out, there exists a "Comrades Court" made up of retirees that never resolve anything or who aggravate the injustices.

In 1985, we realized that it was impossible to continue living in this manner. My first husband's parents wanted to buy us a cooperative apartment.[3] On May 13, 1985 we went to sign up on a waiting list to get one. May 13, 1992, seven years later—in the meantime I had changed husbands—I telephoned this entity, which is called the Department of Cooperative Housing Construction. The woman told me, "You are not one of the people who are considered high priority." The priority people are sick, mentally ill, or others. In April 1992, they allocated apartments to those who signed up in 1984. That year they had 29 apartments at their disposal, to be allocated on a priority basis to repatriated military personnel from Germany. For a city of 9 million people where hundreds of thousands still live in communal accommodations.

It's because of the social housing that is in the process of being constructed in the most distant working-class areas of Moscow. It takes about an hour and a half to get there from the center of town.

The possibility of buying on the open market is a recent development, but the prices are beyond most people. Before, a cooperative studio cost 4,000 rubles, a two room 12,000 rubles, and a three room 18,000 rubles, the equivalent of two Moskvich cars. One paid 40 percent right away and then the rest progressively. In 1992, a studio already cost 200,000 rubles, a two room 500,000, and so on and so forth.

In 1993, prices were already calculated in dollars, actually in tens of thousands of dollars. Home buying is practically impossible.

To get out of our communal apartment, we found a girl who had several small apartments, one for her mother, one for her, plus a third where she lived with a third person whom she married. She agreed to the exchange but it didn't resolve the problem because we had four families and not three. Because one cannot leave a kommunalka unless the situation is resolved for everybody and above all everybody has to be in agreement, which is incredibly rare.

We spent 15 years solving the problem, today the big apartments are of interest to businesses or companies but in the '80s nobody wanted them.

We finally found a solution that suited everyone. The girl did not have enough apartments "to trade," but she finally accepted to move out while keeping an enclave, an old man who was a guard at the Ministry of Railroads. A leftover from the NKVD, he was in charge of verifying the permits at the ministry.

In order to persuade our savior, we convinced her that he didn't have a long time to live. But it's been three years since they've been there and he's still alive.

In deep chagrin at his presence, the family that had moved out, very rich Jewish musicians, succeeded in transforming this apartment into a palace but there's still this enclave, and the smell of old gruel that the old man prepares for himself. Over the period of our long negotiations I developed a friendship with the wife Klara, and I know that they'd decided to have a third child in order to occupy the room when the old man died. Otherwise they risk having someone else move in....

Today, I'm still officially registered in the apartment, in fact I no longer live there, I live in a separate apartment. But I still have the feeling of being condemned to live in a communal apartment. That's the case with my mother; she's not young enough to fling herself into the adventure of solitude. In theory she always has the desire to have an apartment to call her own, but she believes it less and less, she won't know how to organize it, how to clean it....

CHAPTER 26

# The English Girl and the Blackmarketeer

I, Anna Blundy, was fifteen when I first went to Russia in 1985. I met Dima on Red Square at midnight. It was about minus fifteen, startlingly cold, the sky black with sharp stars, and my friend and I weren't dressed for it, skidding around in thin shoes on the thick ice. I thought Dima was Italian at first, he was so well-dressed, an olive green great coat, no hat, and even his shoes looked Western—purple, tassled loafers!

He was 22 and trying to get close to the glamour and danger of the West by dealing hard currency on the black market, selling caviar, laquered boxes, badges of Lenin—the usual tourist stuff.

He came up and asked me for a cigarette, followed me and my friend back to the hotel and stayed the night, picking out words from a phrase book and drinking vodka. I fell in love, I suppose, partly with his dark eyes, but mostly with Russia—no color, no distraction, no advertising, shops or cafes, just itself. I ran away from the tour group I was with, staying at the Hotel Cosmos[1] where Dima[2] could get in, posing as a foreigner with some kind of fake pass, shouting loudly in what he thought might sound like English. Sometimes he got caught by the KGB who hung out in the Soliaris Bar and then he'd be beaten up and kicked out, or arrested, or both. We were together for a week, I think. He even came to Leningrad with us, with our tour group, and he and I were followed everywhere by the KGB. We knew it but I was so young that I don't think I realized how serious it might have been. I loved it, actually. And someone told me that if they wanted to follow you so that you couldn't see them, they would. If you could tell you were being followed, then they were just trying to make a point. Now I wonder if we really were followed, or if it was just Dima's Soviet paranoia.

I went back to England feeling a hundred years older than I had a week earlier, assuming it was all over, but longing for the... exoticism... perhaps of the world behind the Iron Curtain. But Dima had his own fantasies and projections, and he called me from Moscow's central post office all the time, queuing for hours for an international line. He would tell me about the problems he had had with the police because of me, told me that he loved me, and asked me to come join him. I think the police probably knew him, actually. He had already been in prison, he said, or in the cells for the night, perhaps.

I went back to Russia, to Moscow, a few times on school trips and tourist trips and sometimes he was there, sometimes not, but the innocence of the first time I'd met him never really came back. Then, in 1990, in my year off from Oxford studying languages, I was supposed to go and live and work in Russia for a year, and I asked him to find me a flat. I arrived actually off the Trans-Siberian express from Beijing, and he had found me a room in a kommunalka. I spent almost a year in it, God help me. We drank too much and, once, a discarded cigarette set fire to the bed and I woke up to see the whole room on fire. Dima called me "Anna, kotoraya prolila maslo," Anna who spilt the cooking oil, a reference to Bulgakov's Master and Margarita and the small accident of the hapless Anna that sets off a series of phantasmagorical, diabolical events. I think I believed all the horror of Moscow at the very end of Communism was somehow my fault. My father, a journalist, had just been shot dead in El Salvador and life seemed full of fear.

I paid a stodgy woman with that ubiquitous Soviet meringue hair 600 rubles a month for one of her rooms. It was an enormous amount of money at the time, triple the average monthly salary and certainly a lot more than I was earning at my job at the magazine, *New Times*. But my landlady, Zinaida Petrovna, had power over us because, technically, under the terms of my visa, she could have got me arrested for staying in a private apartment. She spied on our every move, all of the comings-and-goings of Dima's friends who became more and more shady and whom I like less and less as law and order disintegrated around us.

As well as, Zinaida Petrovna, we shared the kommunalka with a very old woman and a 30-something couple who I almost never saw. Dima, who was already quite a Mafioso with a bag of foreign currency under the bed, was very frightened of everything. He forbade me to talk to anybody in the house. "Annushka, don't answer if you are asked questions, don't talk about your life, you are running risks you don't understand. They are not people, Toad [his nickname for me]. They are wolves," he would tell me all the time. I doubt if it was even true by then, but he'd grown up and been in trouble under Communism so he brought all the baggage with him.

The kommunalka was completely infested with rats. I would hear them squeaking and gnawing at the metal grating in the floor and inside the actual walls in the night. I was too scared even to go to the toilet in the night when Dima wasn't there. I was terrified of the rats, of running into the old, toothless and horrible-smelling old lady. She had a bad leg, and at night I heard her drag it along the wooden corridor floor, muttering to herself.

We rarely even met in the kitchen, thank God. I used a kettle I'd brought from London in my room, and I killed the rats with poison from London too. They died of thirst, scrabbling at the bath, toilet, and water pipes. The old lady smoked like a chimney. A young man called Aliosha used to come once a week with bread and cigarettes for her, and it was him Dima thought I oughtn't to talk to, that he was some kind of informer. A dying breed by then, surely. The old woman never went out once in a year, and she smoked "Dymok," the cheapest cigarettes, unbelievably strong.

Quite often the shortages were so bad that Aliosha just came round to say sorry there wasn't anything that week, that we should try and buy her the German food aid that had gone straight on to the black market—cornflakes and ready meals that you had to add eggs to, not that there were any eggs and, anyway, the instructions were in German. I felt sorry for her and hated her at the same time. She was not an endearing old lady. She was crabby and frightening. Dima bought me a hamster, and she looked after it once and killed it by feeding it salami all day. I once tried to chat to her, to get her to talk about her life under Stalin and all that kind of thing but she had nothing to say. She had had a completely empty life in this room, not noticing anything in particular, not having anything to say about her neighbors, her job, nothing. She had never even been married. I found it hard to believe that her life had been so blank, but I realize now that she was probably suffering from dementia. Maybe her life had been fascinating!

I was working as a translator for *New Times* for 180 rubles per month and tried, apart from my astronomical rent, to live a Russian life as far as possible for Dima's sake. He didn't like going to restaurants that accept foreign credit card only, because he couldn't pay and felt humiliated. I didn't see many foreigners and didn't shop at Beriozkas.[3] There really wasn't much to eat most of the time unless we went to the hotel restaurants in the grey, concrete suburbs where the gangsters hung out, and Dima told me not to speak to anyone. Great.

One morning very early, there was a knock on the door. It was the police. During the night the couple next door had been murdered! With an axe. Apparently, this aspect of it wasn't that odd—axe murders were not that uncommon according to Dima.[4] When I told this story to Russian friends the bit that surprised them about the whole thing was that the police had actually come. The murder was par for the course. The police told us the couple drank a lot and had invited a man who lived in the apartment upstairs to drink with them, and that this neighbor had murdered them. For a Russian to say someone drinks a lot means they really, really drink a lot. An unimaginable amount. The murderer had already been arrested. Dima saw the woman when the body was taken away and apparently her head was cut in half. I was really worried about being arrested for being a foreigner without the right documents to be living there, and Dima told me to pretend to be mute. I am about the least mute person on the planet. But, in fact, we were not even interrogated. They just sealed up the door[5] to that room, and we carried on living there. I had friends in Moscow that I never would have been able to have in London. I would never have been accepted in a circle of English gangsters, even as someone's girlfriend—as soon as I opened my mouth, you could tell where I came from, that I was posh and university educated. But here nobody could classify me, apart from to think that I must be from another planet. I felt as if I was whenever I talked about London, Oxford, college balls, and going to America with my dad. When the smells in the kommunalka started making me actually throw up, I realized I was pregnant, and I left for London and had an abortion. I was still nineteen, I think. Or twenty maybe. It was that famous winter where there was nothing to eat in Moscow, people were fainting with hunger in Leningrad, and Dima came home in the middle of the night with cardboard boxes full of bread and cooked chicken that a friend of his had stolen from a hotel kitchen for us.

Maybe because we were both sad about the abortion, or maybe because we were both very intoxicated by the mystery of the other's nationality, we decided to get married. I was horrible and backed out at the last minute telling him it was because he didn't know what the last line of Casablanca was, a cultural impossibility. He said, "What's Casablanca?" I said, "Exactly."

Dima had trained as an architect, and he was a really talented artist. When he was not thinking about money, he did wonderful drawings. But as soon as he smelled money he would change, even the look on his face changed. He had these horrible friends—they were armed, they met in shitty hotels, traveled to Vladivostock to pick up cars stolen, and shipped from Europe to then resell in Moscow. In 1991, they were already driving Mercedes, which was very rare in Moscow where the only foreign car on the roads until really recently had been the British Ambassador's purple Jaguar.

The most disturbing thing about his friends was really how nice they were to me, asking me about Margaret Thatcher and trying to practice their English. You want gangsters to be scarred villains but, obviously, things aren't as simple as that.

I came back to Moscow in 1992, and I work for ABC news as a desk assistant—just making coffee and answering phones, doing bits of translating. I also sing in a blues band but I am going to leave soon, I think I'm worn out by this country. I'm going out with an American journalist and haven't told Dima I'm here. Maybe I'll call him.

CHAPTER 27

# An Officer in the Strategic Nuclear Forces

> He answered, "I can't, comrade. I'd be glad to do it, but I can't. It isn't my responsibility. It's a communal apartment. And a fixed price has been set for the bathroom."
>
> —Mikhail Zoshchenko. "The Crisis"
> (*Nervous People and Other Satires*)

I spent my earliest childhood in a communal apartment near Severomorsk, not far from Murmansk.[1] My father was an officer in the Baltic Fleet. Four officer families shared this four-room apartment, situated in social housing but very spacious with a long corridor.

We lived there for five years from 1963 to 1968. The inhabitants were fairly nice, first of all there were no old people, everyone was between 35 and 40 years of age, and then everyone was an officer so there was a professional solidarity, everyone was from the same background. The neighbor took me to kindergarten, the wives prepared meals together.

But in the North men drink a lot, I remember the permanent drunkenness of the apartment's inhabitants, mainly from the two bachelor officers.

Then my father was transferred first to another garrison then to Moscow where he bought a cooperative apartment.

In 1985, I was a young navy officer, a lieutenant. I also left for the North and also lived in a kommunalka with my wife and little daughter.

Based in the Vidaevo garrison, not far from Murmansk, I was in charge of the missiles on board a nuclear submarine.

The whole coast is sprinkled with bays, and there is a garrison in each bay. I can't say how many nuclear submarines there were, it's a military secret. I lived there from 1985 to 1990.

The first year, I lived in a communal apartment. Sailors lived on the base while officers lived in town and were picked up each morning by trucks. The base was 16 kilometers from the city where we lived. It was a big apartment, fairly dirty. We were a lot of officers, we got along well, but the wives argued. Mine had a hard time handling this life, inasmuch as our daughter suffered from the northern climate and was always sick.

To leave the garrison, you needed a special authorization from the commandant. Food products were difficult to find, we were provided with basic supplies once a month. Otherwise in town we could basically find bread and fish, halibut destined for export. We went to buy the fish at a sovkhoz.

Impossible to get vodka. This was in 1985, Gorbachev had just passed the "dry law," and the situation was dramatic, not a drop anywhere. But on board the submarine we had 90 degree alcohol, which was used to clean machines, the hydraulic equipment. I was chosen to be responsible for the alcohol depot because I drank less than the others. Thanks to this position, I was able to have an individual apartment.

In 1986, it was extremely cold, the heating system at the base had broken, the women and children had to be evacuated. That winter it was −35° Celsius, and in the apartment, it was unbearable.

In the North alcohol is called "shilo," which comes from the popular saying "shilo na milo" literally "an awl[2] on the soap." Alcohol in the North is a bartering tool, nobody wants money, and everything is paid for in alcohol.

I cheated. In the fleet, alcohol is measured in kilos while a container holds a liter which is a little less than a kilo of alcohol. So I had at my disposal a small amount and I gave it to those who asked me, obviously in trade for a service or products.

In any case, the commandant himself participated in this trafficking because he controlled the alcohol reserves as a last resort. When an officer from High Command arrived for an inspection, the superior officers always went fishing in one of the area's innumerable lakes, and obviously they needed alcohol to make the fishing party more agreeable...they fished for trout, salmon. In the winter, they went ice fishing.

During the winter, we could do nothing to fix the heating. But during the thaw, I became acquainted with the officer in charge of supplying the garrison with energy. He told me that the workers refused to fix the heating system in such cold, and that they had to be given alcohol. This fellow who was in charge, he didn't have any alcohol. Meanwhile my wife threatened not to come back, she told me that she could no longer live in such cold and in such an apartment. So I went to see the officer in charge of lodging, I told him that I could get him lots of alcohol but that I needed an individual apartment.

He gave me an apartment in exchange for 15 liters of alcohol. This was in 1986. Then the workers did their job for a fee of 10 liters of pure alcohol. One month later the heating system was working and I was living alone! My wife and my daughter came back.

This business gave me some problems. At the time there was still a "zampolit,"[3] an assistant to the commandant who was in charge of political questions and ethics. An individual apartment had to be merited. The zampolit, who was a member of the special housing commission, awarded them (individual apartments) to officers who had particularly distinguished themselves onboard submarines.

Since I didn't have a chance to be counted among those officers, not because I served badly—no on the contrary at the time I led a combat unit—but because I was "Party-less" and in 1986 that was very bad for privileges, there were only about a dozen people who did not have a communist Party card.

The zampolit was furious that I had succeeded in getting an individual apartment, but he was not able to get much further because it was already Perestroika, Glasnost, and his position no longer had much importance, he had even become a little suspect. Ten years earlier, under Brezhnev, I would have had worse problems.

My wife and I were the only people who were very young in a building reserved for officers of the highest rank, my wife was very happy.

In 1989, High Command made me an offer to continue my career in Moscow, one does not refuse such an offer. I was a captain-lieutenant. I had an interview with the head of executive services; he told me, "Who are you?" I tried to answer but he interrupted me, "You are nothing if you are not a Communist." It was an insistent invitation to join the Communist Party; it was strange, it seems so long ago and yet so recent.

Because my daughter was sick—she suffered from anemia and in Murmansk I couldn't get her better—I was obliged to comply, it was absolutely necessary that I return to Moscow. So I joined the Communist Party in the beginning of 1990, as anachronistic as that may seem.

We lived at my parents, but relations were strained in the beginning between my mother and my wife. I was obliged to look for an apartment, but my Moscow salary was much lower than in the North. My wife was a building engineer but she could not find work, on top of which she did not have a "propiska" and my parents refused to have her register at their place.

The result, we got divorced.

I understood then that the army would not take care of me, that I was nothing but a little cog in this administration, and that High Command did not give a fig about my apartment, the conditions I lived in, my family. If I had been called to Moscow by the Ministry of Defense, I would have been put on a waiting list but as I had been nominated by the commander-in-chief of the Navy, I didn't appear on any list.

So I decided to leave the armed forces. In April 1991, I resigned both from the army and from the naval High Command. But what is strange, is that I didn't know how to do it, I sent a written request to leave the Party and nobody paid attention, then I asked to be seen and nobody answered me, it was already anarchy... So I stopped paying my Party dues, and I understood that I had to act in a way to discredit myself as a High Command executive.

I was earning three times less than in Murmansk where my salary had been just enough. So during the day I was an officer in the Soviet Navy's High Command in Moscow and at night I was a bodyguard... I managed a group of eight security guards, we protected important Russian "businessmen." We had to deal with several attacks, mainly in warehouses. To be honest, I worked for "shady" men involved in the black economy.

I was able to continue working for the Navy and the mafia for four months. I still have friends today who do that sort of work and who stayed in the Navy. In any case, at High Command there's practically nothing else to do.

Still looking for accommodations, I found a woman who had a room in a communal apartment that she didn't live in. With a "white" marriage, I was able to move into this room in an old building not far from the Kursk train station. Two rooms were occupied by two old people from the same family, and a third by a single mother who lived without her child. I had very good relations with the grandmothers, but the girl was very high-strung and very aggressive with me, a really nasty person. She pretended to need all four burners on the stove at once just to annoy me.

This girl didn't work, she had some Armenian and Azerbaijan friends who spent longish periods in her room, and left her money.

That was when I met Olga, she lived in the suburbs and worked in a joint venture in the center of town. I fell crazily in love with her, she was a ravishing woman with a lot of charm. I invited her to come live with me, to avoid her daily three hour commute.

This was in the autumn of 1992, I was no longer working at headquarters nor at my bodyguard business, I was in charge of a Russian-German company that exported wood. I often traveled, tasked to accompany the wood.

Last summer I found myself in Novorossisk[4] where I had to organize a boat to go to Syria. Olga was at my place. Normally when I wasn't there she'd go back to her place, but she had worked late at the office, a Russian-American publishing joint venture.

As it was summer, the elderly ladies had gone to their dacha.[5] So Olga was alone with Joanna, my hysterical neighbor who is about 24 years old. In the morning Joanna woke up in a bad mood and wanted to chase Olga out of the house, telling her that she had no right to be there and that she would call the militia. Olga answered that she should mind her own business and pretended that nothing had happened and then Joanna seized an enormous glass jar[6] and broke it over her head.

Her head all bloody, Olga called an ambulance and the police, who announced that it was part of daily life and impossible to file a claim. Nonetheless a policeman told her that if she insisted, for 10,000 rubles, he could make things unpleasant for the girl. Olga was in such a state that she didn't have time for revenge. She was taken to the hospital where she remained for a long time. Her forehead was badly sewn up and the wound had to be opened up because pieces of glass remained inside.

The worst was that my relations with Olga deteriorated after this event. This beautiful girl now has a scar that disfigures her a bit, she has to have bangs to cover her forehead, and she bears a grudge against me. Our relationship continued for a bit but it was out of the question that she come to my place. And then she reproached me for something, maybe she wanted me to give the woman a good beating. But I can't beat a woman.

I tried for a while to find alternative apartments for the elderly ladies and the girl but I quickly grew discouraged. I preferred to sell everything, I had some beautiful antique furniture, a car, video cameras, and I bought a little apartment from two old drunks. I'm in the midst of redoing the whole interior, it was in an unbelievably filthy state when I arrived.

I don't have Olga any more but I also no longer have neighbors....

CHAPTER 28

# From Putsch to Putsch

> At least some kind-hearted person told him of a small room about three yards square in size.
>
> —Alexey Tolstoy. *The Viper*

The first time that a delegation from the Comrades Court came to see me, they told me, "Tatiana N., you cannot continue to receive so many foreigners at your place, your neighbor is complaining, she is afraid of being spied on because she works in a top secret factory for the Ministry of Defense..."

It was in 1985, in the first few months of my stay in a communal apartment situated just behind the White House in Moscow.[1] I didn't really mind sharing, I wanted to live in the center of town, I make musical programs for television, and above all I didn't want to live in the suburbs.

I share the apartment with V. and E. V. is about 30, he's an ex-military fellow from Ukraine, who managed to get himself registered in Moscow as a "limitchik"—limitchiki were people who got a residency permit thanks to a work contract. He left the military two years ago, now he's a mechanic in our building's courtyard, he fixes cars for the neighborhood's inhabitants, it's a sort of private business, and obviously he doesn't pay taxes...

He lives in the room opposite mine, sometimes he puts up a girl for a month or two, never longer, and he says afterward that they annoy him.

E., she's 54 years old, she's never been married and doesn't have any children. But she has a lover, 20 years her elder, communist like her. She is an industrial draughtsman, she works in a factory that was secret for a long time.

The kommunalka is a product of the Soviet regime, which generated a culture of hatred, it's unique in the world. One can't even say that it's an awful lifestyle; it's more accurate to say that it's peculiar. It's a very peculiar lifestyle.

E. has always hated me, she has no friends, other than her sister, and she never receives anyone. She'd seen all my jazz musician friends leave for Holland, Great Britain, Denmark, in the '80s... These were all the people tied to my work, who came to Moscow to record programs, it was the beginning of Perestroika, they stayed in my second room, we spoke English deep into the night... Many times she lodged a complaint against me. Every two or three years, she went in with her little letter of denunciation...

We have a completely different schedule, she goes off to work at 7:30 while I'm still asleep. As for me I often come back at dawn, because I have programs very late at night. More than once I heard her say, "Here's the whore who's come back to sleep."

Everything according to her was my fault: the dirt in the apartment, the cockroaches in the kitchen. The difference between me and her is that when I clean I do it mainly for myself, whereas when she cleans she says it's for others... She never scrubs the toilets, it's always me who has to do it. In revenge, when she uses the toilet she lifts the seat to show that she doesn't want to use the same toilet as me. She only cleans her half of the kitchen, in fact she doesn't even have the right to a portion of the kitchen because she's the only one registered here whereas in the beginning I moved in with my son and my ex-husband.

When the first "putsch" occurred in August 1991, I was petrified because on Monday morning I'd just heard on the radio that Gorbachev was deposed, those cretins were in power, *Swan Lake* was on television. I saw myself arrested, no more jazz, no more freedom, obviously it was far from being the reality, but it was something that was coming up from deep inside me, my childhood no doubt, an unspeakable fright.

In the kitchen I saw V. He told me that it was all the same to him, as long as there was merchandise in the stores. At the time, stores were empty.

My apartment was invaded by my friends from Finnish television, we were close to the White House, they'd just come from filming pro-Yeltsin demonstrations, all of Moscow's intelligentsia was in the streets, it was emotional, such intelligent people.

E., she did not want to be outdone. She disappeared the morning of the putsch, Monday, August 19, 1991, she came back four days later, she walked around the apartment saying, "Hum, obviously, there's a mess as usual in here." She wanted to be far away from the White House, at the time it was Yeltsin's stronghold. She and her lover are Stalinists, they love order more than anything else, but I don't understand why they never managed to leave this apartment. He's had money for a couple of years now, with the furs he buys her he could have moved her into a cooperative (private) apartment, there are mysteries in E.'s life...

And there was the second putsch, Rutzkoi's and Khasbulatov's.[2] When Yeltsin dissolved Parliament on September 21, 1993, the crowd of communists and fascists began crowding around in front of my windows—I live on the ground floor, and this time I was the one who left. Our telephone was cut off, during the first putsch I called all my friends in Vilnius,[3] we spoke of "their parliament," of Soviet tanks in 1991. This time I couldn't even call, and I was surrounded by drunken Communists. I preferred to leave. And that's not even mentioning that they were always banging on our door. "Open up, we are the White House defenders, we want to wash and to eat." I was most decidedly not comfortable, they were not really "my people."

E. she stayed. I think she was tricked because Sunday, October 3rd, they all thought that they were about to win, she and her pals, the Communists and the Fascists.

V. was also there, spoke a little to me; he told me that he slept on the floor because he was afraid of being shot through the window. There were some people who died in the building, there were plenty of snipers everywhere.

When I came back to the house on October 7th, three days after the crushing of the parliamentary rebellion, E. didn't say anything to me. We never spoke of politics; in fact, we never spoke except to yell every two or three years. But I saw signs of gunshots on her window, I don't even know how she lived through those days when the fate of our country was decided, even though I've lived under the same roof as she for the last 11 years, we've shared the same bathroom and the same kitchen...

Regarding our kitchen, I have an anecdote. Last year some Dutch friends who were staying with me greeted me one evening saying,

"Tanyusha, we've a surprise for you. Come into the kitchen." I let out a shriek seeing that they'd put the table in the kitchen which is never done in a kommunalka and that they had, even more dramatically, taken E.'s plates and a casserole belonging to V.

"Miserable ones, what have you done? You're crazy, you're in a communal apartment!" I said to them. "Well, in the Netherlands we too, we have communes!" they answered.

After returning to Amsterdam, they wrote me to apologize. They understood the difference between "commune" and "kommunalka."

Now I'd really like to leave. Not really because of the kommunalka because if I have a sense of privacy, I don't have a problem with the accommodation. It doesn't bother me to share, even with an old communist like E. But I can't stand this White House that has become black, any longer, this horrible building which has always been an architectural sacrilege and which is becoming the symbol of this absurd battle for a power, whatever it might be, that still deceives us.

CHAPTER 29

# Seventeen Years after the Fall of the USSR

> Why, why, why, he answers, just let me rent out my room for seventy rubles, then I won't need anything from you.
> —Ludmilla Petrushevskaya. *The time—night*

My name is Anna Ivanovna Rudenko, I am of Ukrainian heritage, I received Russian citizenship thanks to my last husband who is now deceased.

This is a 147-square-meter apartment and 4 families live here, or 16 people in total. Currently, in 2008, we're 11 permanent residents, the 5 other inhabitants are registered here but don't live here.

As for me, for more than 20 years I've been living in this 22-square-meter room, I'm living here "illegally," that is without being registered in Moscow since 1987, and for eight years I've been the owner. I bought it in exchange for another room that I had elsewhere.

I share this room with my daughter, my son-in-law, and my grandson Andrei who's 12. I sleep on the sofa that you see over there, my daughter and son-in-law on the balcony, and my grandson on a bed that we converted under the little desk where he does his homework. Right now he's at his English lesson, he'll be back shortly. We try and keep him occupied after school as much as possible because he's very active and hates this room where the four of us live, as well as the wardrobe and the refrigerator because we are not allowed to have a refrigerator in the kitchen, each family has one in its room. Andrei also does karate.

Lida, the neighbor, who you saw just now in the kitchen has lived here since 1976, she and her husband have one room and her mother-in-law has another, they're lucky to have two. There's another room that is 16 square meters, which is shared by a family of five.

In the mid-1990s, there was a lot of housing commotion, many developers threw themselves into privatizing communal apartments, at the time they were buying them for very little, $5,000–$10,000 maximum, I heard talk of a case where they succeeded in grabbing a room in exchange for one or two cases of vodka, that's without even mentioning the rumors, true or false, of killing retirees in order to get their rooms.

Once all of the rooms were bought up, the developers renovated and rented them, the big apartments in the center of the city rented for up to $10,000–$15,000 per month to expatriates or to rich Georgians or Armenians who came to do business in Moscow.

At that time obviously we too, we were fair game for developers who one after another tried to privatize the apartment, sure we were on the ground floor and people don't like the ground floor, but the building is extraordinary with all the molding and exterior sculptures, and then it looks out on "*Chistye Prudi*" "clear ponds," it's one of the most prestigious areas in Moscow's historical center, not far from the Kremlin.

But at the time there was a woman who didn't want to leave, and it was enough to have one refusal to block everything, the apartment could not be privatized unless everyone accepted the exchange or the proposed amount of money. This woman died four years ago, but now we have very few offers, it's true too that in our area the price of a square meter is up to $14,000–$16,000, nobody's bought out for a case of vodka and who's going to pay $1.5 million for an apartment where everything needs to be redone, developers aren't crazy!

Me, I'm fine here, I'm 75 years old, and I often receive friends in my room, I play the guitar and also I'm quite well known for my herbal medicinal skills, I bring herbs from Poltava in Ukraine, it's 14 hours by train from here, and I practice homeopathy. I help certain teachers prepare mixtures, but I don't like to work, me I like to sleep, to rest, go out, take a walk. I don't like the Internet, I like to read, and I try to prevent my grandson from spending too much time in front of that computer when he comes back from school. My son-in-law is an allergist, they just opened their little clinic with my daughter, but they don't make enough money to buy an apartment.

Before it was very jolly here, we celebrated the New Year all together, now it's each one for themselves, it's a sign of the times. In the building there are people who earn fortunes and live in apartments that are the same size but which are for one family, me I have a pension of 5,000 rubles per month which is $200, how can you make a comparison? But I'm not complaining, I'm a happy woman, I had three husbands, and I have a lot of friends; money one can always borrow, friends not. I think I am the happiest of women.

CHAPTER 30

# Two Sisters through History

> Are you aware of the resolution of August 12 which exempted my apartment from any of your consolidations or tenant transfers?
> We are, answered Shvonder.
>
> —Mikhaïl Bulgakov. *Heart of a Dog*

My name is Nina Vitalievna Sheremetsinskaia, I was brought here from the maternity hospital where I was born in 1927, and I have never moved. My sister Elena who you see is six years younger than me, she was an astronomer and worked her entire life in secret aviation factories, they called them *"iashchiki,"* "drawers," she drew astronomical charts for the pilots. In the beginning, there were five members of my family in this one room, then we got a second room.

Before the Revolution, this apartment was inhabited by a rich English family, and so we inherited an English gas stove, there was little gas to be had at the time, most had coal stoves. We kept warm with coal anyway, and my parents didn't let me go out of the room when I was small because there was a crazy woman who chopped wood on the floor in the hallway; in these apartments, there were always axes and one day, it could've ended badly.

After the war we were up to 20 people living here, the atmosphere has always been very peaceful even if we had some unfortunate occurrences, notably with a prostitute who lived in the room where a young theater actress lives now, Olga Logvinenko, her husband and their little

3-year-old son. But Olga is expecting a second child and no doubt they're going to leave, inasmuch as the little one is often sick because of the dust mites in the wallpaper and in the floor, she has to wash the floor every day and despite everything the little one suffers from allergies. And then it's overheated with those gigantic radiators, which date back to before the war when it was still −40 degrees in winter.

They have a buyer who lives nearby and who is interested in their room so he can house the woman who looks after his son, he's a television producer, he's offering them $230,000 for a 20-square-meter room but with $230,000 these days in Moscow you can no longer buy a two-room in a decent area, this is Chaplygina Street, you go down the street and you have the Tabakov Theater,[1] the Estonian Embassy which is always guarded so, for sure, you can take a walk at night when it's hot.

Lots of inhabitants have left, Nadezhda Konstantinovna even though she had a tiny pension, Alexander Fedorovich who was in the military. Five families left and were replaced by three, and my sister and I succeeded in getting the three rooms that we occupy today. There is a fifth and sixth room where people are registered, but we don't see them often, they don't live here permanently.

Our parents were teachers, of math and physics, I was an engineer in my working life. I was enrolled in the Communist Party, not my younger sister. In our childhood, we liked the international atmosphere, which prevailed in the building, the famous polar explorer Krenkel lived here, there were only intelligent and cultured people here, mainly teachers, so we never experienced denunciations here.

We never got married and don't have children, so we didn't want to leave and don't want to now. Our outpatient clinic is on the corner of the street, the subway as well. For the young, it's perhaps tempting, but for old people it is very difficult to change areas.

Since the apartments were privatized and renovated, we've had the good luck to see decent people, not bandits, move into our building: our neighbors are a banker, a businesswoman, there are also Germans who recently bought. These are very well brought-up people, their children help us carry packages when they meet us in the stairway.

We've kept a lot of canned goods, some are from before the war, all are stamped. We use them sometimes.

# Appendix A

*Appendix A, B, and C have been published in 1929 in the the daily* KRASNAYA GAZETA *(The Red Gazette), a daily newspaper, at different periods an organ of the central, provincial, city committees of the All-Union Communist Party (of Bolcheviks) and the Petrograd/Leningrad Soviet. It circulated from January 1918 until February 1939.*

### Enforced Requisitioning of Excess Living Space
### Draft Resolution of the Regional Executive Committee

Yesterday at a meeting of the grand presidium of the Regional Executive Committee, the following draft resolution was adopted concerning the requisitioning of excess living space.

We quote it in its entirety.

"In view of the acute housing crisis in the city of Leningrad and the necessity to provide living space to demobilized military personnel, to students, to persons evicted from apartment houses threatened by destruction, and to workers without living space, and changing the current regulations concerning excess living space, the presidium of the Leningrad Soviet resolves:

Rooms beyond the living space allotted to the family of a tenant and those provided for occupational reasons or due to illness are to be considered excess rooms.

Entire excess rooms are subject to being requisitioned from tenants in accordance with administrative procedures and to being transferred to the exclusive control of the district communal offices for the settlement of the above-named categories of workers.

In the requisitioning of excess rooms, persons of different gender may not be forcibly settled in the same room with the exception of spouses and of children younger than 12 years of age.

Tenants are given the choice of rooms remaining to them within the limits of point 1 or the right in the course of three weeks to settle rooms requisitioned from them with inhabitants of their choice on condition that the latter have given over to the district communal offices the rooms previously occupied by them or in general rooms suitable for living in exchange for those subject to requisition.

Complaints concerning the improper requisitioning of living space are to be filed within a week to the presidium of the district Soviet; filing of a complaint suspends the requisitioning.

Procedures for the requisitioning of excess rooms are set by instructions to be published in the course of development of this resolution."

In discussion of this question, it was revealed that according to a study by the Regional Statistical Office, there are in Leningrad up to 700 thousand square meters of excess living space within rooms and about 15 thousand rooms paid for as excess living space. In the present housing crisis, it is understandable that it is necessary to take all measures to receive in one way or another these excess living spaces to alleviate the housing needs. This draft of a resolution of the Regional Executive Committee foresees precisely this requisitioning of excess living space.

Yesterday this draft resolution was urgently sent for the approval of the Presidium of the All-Russian Central Executive Committee.

\* \* \*

In all frankness it has to be recognized that this decision of the presidium of the District Executive Committee is the only way to alleviate the housing crisis in the immediate future. The unpleasant aspect for many of this decision, specifically the enforced reduction in living space and the enforced settlement of residents, is strongly mitigated by the three-week period during which tenants can settle premises with persons of their own choosing. These persons only have to transfer their own vacated living space to the district communal offices. It is assumed that many who take advantage of this privilege in a timely manner will not experience any unpleasant consequences for themselves in the upcoming reduction of living space.

The resolution will take legal effect immediately after approval of it by the Presidium of the All-Russian Central Executive Committee.

# Appendix B

**New Procedure for the Settlement, Voluntary Reduction in Living Space and Re-Planning of Apartments**

The Presidium of the Leningrad City Soviet yesterday published a compulsory order according to which **all vacated living space** (apartments, rooms, etc.) **is to be transferred to the apartment house managements for distribution by the district housing bureaus that have been organized anew.** This regulation applies both to apartment houses under the trusts of communal apartment houses as well as to ZhAKT (Housing Lease Cooperative Society) properties in which all members of the ZhAKT and their families have living space of not less than 7 square meters per person.

Tenants vacating entire rooms in the course of voluntary reduction in living space have the right to settle them **at their discretion** with persons from among the workers, but on the condition that those populating these rooms have provided certification **of the release of their prior rooms to the District Housing Bureau.** Voluntary reduction in living space within rooms is permitted only if there is an excess of living space of more than 4 and a half square meters for each new resident.

All space that comes under the administration of the District Housing Bureau will be distributed first of all among very needy workers in industry and transportation, demobilized Red Army soldiers, and persons evicted from housing that is a public safety threat.

The numerous lawsuits will end between tenants and apartment house managements that have occurred due to the lack of a clear regulation concerning at whose expense work on the re-planning of apartments should be made in a reduction of living space. The Presidium of the Leningrad City Soviet yesterday confirmed a regulation that **the Regional Housing Authority will assume all costs of re-planning apartments, but at the same time all space vacated as a result of the re-planning will also be settled through the District Housing Bureaus.**

# Appendix C

**Forced Reduction in Space of Apartments**

Previously (*Krasnaya Gazeta* No. 236) we published the draft of a resolution of the presidium of the Regional Executive Committee concerning the forced reduction of living space of residents in apartments. The draft of the resolution was sent for approval to the All-Russian Central Executive Committee.

**Let us recall briefly the main provisions of the draft:**

Rooms beyond the living space allotted according to current norms to the family of a tenant and those provided for occupational reasons or due to illness are to be considered excess rooms.

Excess rooms are subject to requisitioning from tenants according to administrative procedure and to transfer to the exclusive control of the district communal office for the settlement of workers.

In the requisitioning of excess rooms, persons of different gender may not be forcibly settled in the same room with the exception of spouses and of children younger than 12 years of age.

Tenants are given the choice of rooms remaining to them or the right in the course of three weeks to settle rooms subject to requisition from them with inhabitants of their choice on condition that the latter have given over to the district communal offices the rooms previously occupied by them or in general rooms suitable for living in exchange for those subject to requisition.

Yesterday a notice of the People's Commissariat for Internal Affairs was received in which it is stated that the People's Commissariat for Internal Affairs considers it necessary in view of the acute housing crisis in Leningrad to approve this resolution and to implement it.

Obviously, in the near future the draft will be considered as a final matter in the All-Russian Central Executive Committee.

New Rules Concerning the Use of Living Accommodations.

Yesterday the Department of the Communal Economy sent for the consideration of the presidium of the Leningrad Soviet the draft of an obligatory decree on the re-planning of premises, the exchange of living space and voluntary reduction in living space. Apartment house managements are reminded that under no circumstances should they counteract the production of such internal-apartment re-planning, which is done under technical supervision and leads to the creation of new apartments and rooms. Such re-planning provides the possibility of a more compact and consequently more rational use of living space.

If a tenant carries out re-planning at his own expense, he is given the right to himself settle the rooms resulting from the re-planning.

It is categorically confirmed that apartment house managements do not have the right to prevent the exchange of living space between workers as long as the exchange is not of a speculative nature or the tenant has outstanding debts to the apartment house management.

Tenants may carry out voluntary reduction of excess living space within rooms by themselves without special agreement of the apartment house management. At the same time there must be no less than 5 square meters for every new resident.

# Appendix D

## RULES FOR THE USE OF LIVING ACCOMMODATIONS APPROVED by Resolution of the Council of Ministers of the RSFSR on October 18, 1962 No. 1390

**Maintenance of Living Accommodations**

1. Written contracts are concluded between tenants and housing managements concerning the use of living accommodations on the basis of the approved Model Rental Contract for Living Accommodations in Apartment Houses of Local Soviet of Workers' Deputies, State, Cooperative and Civic Organizations.
2. Renters of living accommodations and persons living with them are obligated to:
    a) use the provided accommodations in accordance with the terms of the rental contract;
    b) use electric energy, water, and gas economically, preventing leaks and mismanagement of their expenditure;
    c) preserve green spaces, children's and sports grounds and apartment house equipment;
    d) keep clean and orderly the rented living accommodations and common spaces;
    e) take immediately upon detection of faults in the apartment measures to repair damages and, where necessary, to report about this to the apartment house management;
    f) comply with fire safety rules regarding furnace stoves and kitchen fires when using electrical, gas and other appliances, not permit the installation of home-made safety fuses;
    g) collect garbage and food waste in special closed cans in the absence in the apartment house of a refuse chute and regularly take them out of the apartment to designated places.
2. Renters of living accommodations and all those persons living with them are forbidden to:
    a) obstruct balconies, hallways, corridors, stairways and emergency exits;

b) keep in apartments objects and substances that pollute the air;
   c) produce in apartments things that cause damage to the facilities or disrupt normal living conditions for the inhabitants;
   d) install on the roofs of apartment houses individual antennas for radios and televisions without permission of the apartment house management.
3. Tenants of living accommodations and members of their families voluntarily participate in activities for the development and preservation of green spaces in the territories adjacent to apartment houses.

Regulations inside Apartments

4. In apartments inhabited by several families, a responsible person for the apartment shall be chosen by the residents, and his instructions relating to the implementation of these Rules shall be obligatory for all persons living in the apartment.
5. Tenants of living accommodations are obligated without obstruction to admit apartment house management personnel and representatives of the civic apartment house committee for inspection of the technical condition and sanitary maintenance of the premises occupied by them.
6. In apartments inhabited by several families, all the residents have equal rights to the use of auxiliary premises and equipment for apartments.
7. From 11 p.m. to 7 a.m. quiet should be maintained in apartments. Use of any kind of speakers during the indicated time can only be permitted under conditions of reduction of volume to the degree that it does not disturb the rest of the inhabitants. Upon leaving the inhabited premises, the owner of the speakers is obligated to turn them off. It is forbidden to use record players, radios, and other installations with speakers on balconies or window sills with open windows.
8. The procedure for the use of a bathroom in apartments occupied by several families, as well as taking turns for cleaning places used by all, is established by mutual agreement of all the renters of residential premises of the apartment.
9. Cooking food on primus and kerosene stoves is permitted only in the kitchen or in other places designated by the apartment house management.
10. Washing clothes is permitted in bathrooms (but not in bathtubs). In the absence of a bathroom in the apartment, washing clothes is permitted in the kitchen only when food is not being prepared.
11. Cleaning of clothes, carpets, rugs and bedding is permitted only in places designated by the apartment house management.
12. Keeping cats and dogs in separate apartments occupied by a single family is permitted on condition that rules of sanitation and hygiene are observed and in apartments occupied by several families only in addition with the consent of all the residents.

Renovation of Apartments and Their Equipment

13. Tenants of living accommodations are required to carry out at their own expense current repairs of the premises occupied by them and of common areas in apartments. The following are included in current repairs of living accommodations and common areas carried out by tenants at their own expense: whitewashing of ceilings, painting of walls or pasting of wallpaper, painting of floors and doors, of window frames from the inside, painting of window sills, inserting of glass panes, replacement of window and door devices, repair of electric wiring from the point of its entrance into the apartment. At the request of the tenant, repairs can be made by the apartment house management for a fee according to rates that have been approved in the prescribed manner. If the repairs have been necessitated by faulty parts of the building or of the apartment house equipment or are connected with overall repairs of the apartment house, they are carried out at the expense of the apartment house management.
14. Re-equipping and re-planning of living accommodations and common areas, re-arrangement of heating and sanitary devices may take place only with the written permission of the district (city) executive committee of the Soviet of Workers' Deputies.
15. Damage to apartments and to apartment house equipment that has occurred by fault of the residents must be corrected by them or by the apartment house management at the expense of those at fault.
16. Tenants of living accommodations who have permitted unauthorized re-equipping or re-planning of living accommodations and common areas or the re-arrangement of heating and sanitary devices must bring the premises back to their former state at their own expense, and in the event of failure to do so, the cost of doing so up to 10 rubles will be recovered from them according to the procedure prescribed by decree of the Soviet of People's Commissars of the RSFSR of December 28, 1944, No. 857 "On Documents According To Which Recovery of Debts Is Carried Out On the Basis of Executive Endorsements by Notary Offices" (Collection of Decrees of the RSFSR 1945 No.1, Article 1). In those cases where the cost exceeds 10 rubles, recovery from those at fault takes place through filing of a claim through the courts.
17. In the event of a transfer in the prescribed manner of the rights and obligations of a tenant under a lease to a member of his family living together with him in the given premises, a personal financial account in the name of the new tenant will be opened by the apartment house management. Upon leaving the living accommodations for another place of permanent residency for the entire family, the tenant is required to vacate and release to the apartment house management by law the premises occupied by him and its equipment in good condition. It is forbidden to remove equipment and

devices that upon such removal may damage separate construction elements or the decoration of the premises. Damages done by the tenant to the premises, as well as current repairs of the premises not carried out that are the responsibility of the tenant, shall be noted in the written document of vacating of the premises. In this case the cost of the needed repairs and the expenses of the apartment house management to correct the damages caused to the premises shall be paid at the expense of the tenant in the prescribed manner. The written document of vacating of the premises is composed and signed by representatives of the apartment house management and of the civic apartment house committee and by the tenant.

Distribution of Expenses

18. All tenants of residential premises must pay for rent and utilities on time.
19. The distribution of expenses for lighting, heating, repair of common areas, cost of telephone and utilities in apartments occupied by several families takes place as agreed among the tenants of the living accommodations. In the absence of agreement, expenses are distributed as follows:
    a) Payment for electrical energy in residential rooms where there is a common meter—proportional to the strength of lights and small appliances of each tenant;
    b) Payment for heating of residential rooms by a common furnace—according to the amount of space in the heated premises;
    c) Payment for a common telephone—according to the number of persons in the apartment using the telephone, irrespective of the number of phone conversations;
    d) Payment for repairs, lighting of common spaces of an apartment and payment of bills for gas—according to the number of residents (including household helpers, temporary residents and children, regardless of age). If individual residents are absent for over a month, payment for utilities during the time of their absence is not charged. Absent persons are not freed from payment for telephone and heat.
20. Disputes between residents in apartments occupied by several families concerning cleaning of public spaces, allocation of expenses for utilities, or the use of auxiliary premises are decided by civic apartment house committees or by comrades' courts.

Liability for Failure to Comply with the Rules for the Use of Living Accommodations

21. Tenants of living accommodations and persons living with them who violate the Rules for the Use of Living Accommodations are subject to public pressure through apartment house committees and comrades courts.

22. In the event of systematic violation or damage to the occupied premises by tenants or members of their families or systematic violation of the rules of socialist communal life that make living with them in the same apartment or apartment house impossible for others, and if warnings and public pressure have proved ineffective, leases of residential premises are dissolved ahead of time through the courts.

# Notes

**Introduction**

1. Plural form of kommunalka.

## 1   "Uplotnienie": Filling Up

1. Prince Felix Yusupov was one of the participants in the murder of the mad Russian monk Grigory Rasputin in 1916.
2. Ivan Aivazovsky (1817–1900): Russian painter of Armenian origins, famous for his seascapes.
3. In Russian *Narodnyy komissariat vnutrennikh del*. The Soviet secret police acquired a series of names throughout history. Originally called the Cheka, it was subsequently renamed GPU, NKVD, MVD, and KGB (all these abbreviations are mentioned in the interviews).
4. "Neighbor" is the time-honored term. The renters of the kommunalka were the "inhabitants" and among themselves were "neighbors." Nonetheless, they often addressed each other as "neighbor" and not by their name or patronymic.

## 2   White Army, Red Army

1. The "patefon" a distortion of Pathe-phone, the gramophone.

## 3   The Visit to Lenin

1. Before the Revolution, Jews were not allowed to live in the capitals (St. Petersburg and Moscow) when they did not have higher education. On the other hand, they were not allowed to be enrolled in Russia's universities. Consequently only rich families could afford to send their children abroad for education, so that upon their return they could reside in the capital cities.

2. Ilya Repin (1844–1930). Leading Russian painter famous for his portraits of important Russian figures and historical subject matter.
3. Isaac Levitan (1860–1900). Classical Russian landscape painter.
4. Small coinage used in the beginning of the century.
5. Headquarters of Lenin and a famous girls' school before the Revolution.

## 4  Like Life in Naples

1. *Izvestia* was the official newspaper of the Soviet government.
2. *Pravda*, started in 1912 in St. Petersburg and closed by decree in 1991, was the official newspaper of the communist party.
3. Decree of 1918. The "without rights" were close to 5 million people not counting their families.
4. The comparison comes from the interviewee.

## 5  I, Princess Golitsyn

1. Valentin Serov (1865–1911). Russian painter. One of the premier portrait artists of his era.
2. 80 miles northwest of Moscow.
3. Southwestern suburb of Paris.

## 6  Spy Stories

1. Richard Sorge, a master spy, who revealed the number of divisions of the German army and even the date of the German attack to Stalin (Stalin didn't believe him.) condemned to death and executed by the Japanese in 1944.
2. Willy Stahl, like Richard Sorge, was a member of Comintern. Arrested in 1937, he was shot.
3. Russian region on the border with Finland.
4. Communist International (abbreviated as Comintern), also known as the Third International, was an international communist organization founded in Moscow in March 1919.
5. A Soviet military medal.
6. In 1941 Hungary was one of the signatories of the Anti-Comintern Pact, and were involved in numerous actions against the Soviets.

## 7  The Black Crow

1. Nickname for the black van used by the NKVD.

## 8  Even the Baltics

1. A port city on the Black Sea.
2. A port on the Black Sea.
3. A collective farm.
4. A state farm.
5. City named after the prominent Communist party leader Sergei Kirov, whose 1934 assassination launched Stalin's Great Terror.

## 9  The Siege of Leningrad

1. Valery Chkalov (1904–1938). Soviet pilot who was famous for a 63-hour flight over the North Pole.
2. The city of St. Petersburg stands on the Neva river.
3. The "road of life" was the ice road transport route across the frozen Lake Ladoga, which provided the only access to the city during the siege. The total number of people evacuated through the "road of life" was about 1.3 million, mostly women and children.

## 10  The Denunciation

1. A famous square in Moscow with a pond where the Bulgakov novel *The Master and Margarita* opens.
2. Soviet agency that administered the labor camp systems. Generally refers to the camps themselves.
3. The Arbat is a famous pedestrian street in the historical center of the Moscow.
4. The main opera and ballet theater in Moscow.
5. The Shahbanu was Soraya Bakhtiary (1932–2001), the second wife and Queen consort of Mohammad Reza Pahlavi, the last Shah of Iran.

## 11  Summer 1948

1. The famous emblematic black car for the members of the party nomenklatura.
2. Popular resort on the Black Sea coast. The city has been selected to be the host of the Olympic Winter Games in 2014.
3. Vsevolod Meyerhold (1874–1940). Great innovative theatre director who was executed by the Soviet regime.

## 12   The Ambulance, the Dead, and the Others

1. Russian fashion designer born in 1938.
2. Moscow district, home to the Taganka theater, which was founded in 1964 by the famous director Yuri Lyubimov.
3. Pejorative nickname the Russians gave Ukrainians, because of their pronunciation.
4. Many Russians had axes—and still do—to cut firewood. The axe is, unfortunately, a part of many kommunalka stories.
5. An industrial city near Tolstoy's ancestral estate Yasnaya Polyana.

## 13   The American Legacy

1. Russian city on the Volga river, named after Friedrich Engels (1820–1895), German father of communist theory alongside Karl Marx.
2. Republic created following the Russian Revolution. The German invasion of 1941 marked the end of the Volga Republic. In 1941 Stalin issued a Decree of Banishment, which abolished the A.S.S.R. and exiled all Volga Germans to Central Asia and Siberia, fearing they could act as German spies.
3. Kutuzov Prospect is one of the residential thoroughfares leading from the center to the suburbs of the state dachas. Under Brezhnev, members of the government lived there.

## 14   Jewish Poison in the Pots

1. Second-largest city in Uzbekistan, noted for being part of the Silk Road between China and the West. In the fourteenth century it became the capital of the empire of Timur (Tamerlane).
2. Capital of Uzbekistan.
3. In communal apartments, the rooms for collective use are cleaned by the inhabitants by turn and a timetable is usually hung on the kitchen door. It wasn't unusual for certain inhabitants to pay others to do their turn, which created an odd relationship of masters and maids even inside the apartment.
4. The foremost depository of Russian fine art, located in Moscow.
5. One of the main steam baths in Moscow. Baths are a deep-rooted part of the Russian lifestyle.
6. The "anti-cosmopolitan campaign" of 1948, when the Jews were accused of being non-patriotic, culminated with the alleged "Doctor's plot," in which Jewish doctors were charged with having poisoned and mistreated members of the Soviet government. The prosecution of the doctors was ultimately halted by Stalin's death in 1953.
7. Gittis: a famous Moscow theater school.

8. A city on the Volga, now called Samara.
9. "Khrushchoby": nickname for the social buildings built in the '60s by Nikita Khrushchev, with the goal of reducing communal apartments. Play on words with "Trushchoby," that is, "hovel," "reduced." These apartments were often constructed hastily of inferior materials. Situated in suburbs, these accommodations deteriorated quickly but had the merit of being individual.

## 15  The Letter

1. Classic situation. Rooms stayed empty until their "legal" status was resolved that often bordered on the absurd. In certain apartments, entire families squeeze into 12 square meters and cannot use the empty room next door because it does not "belong" to them and is not "registered" to them.
2. Equivalent of Communications Ministry.
3. In Russia, you begin with Grade 1 at age 7 to finish—college-ready—in Grade 10.
4. "Old Bolshevik"; the name for early Bolsheviks who enrolled in the Party before the Revolution and had access to special shops and a whole gamut of privileges.
5. Moscow prison that became famous when the "putschists" of August 1991 were held there for several months.
6. (Author's note) The pieces of the draft, reconstructed and photocopied, were in fact shown to me.
7. A Russian city in the Urals south of Ekaterinburg that was closed to foreigners until 1992.
8. To move out, a kommunalka inhabitant has to find "an exchange" meaning a person who agrees to come and live in his room and gives him in exchange either a room in another kommunalka, or a little individual studio. These "exchanges" were a real obsession for the Soviets for a long time, giving rise to unbelievable tragicomical situations.

## 16  New Year's Eve Celebration

1. A city in the north Caucasus that has been a health resort since 1803.
2. In Soviet Russia, where Christ's birth was not celebrated, trees were decorated—and still are—for New Year's Eve and not for December 25. Grandfather Frost—our Santa Claus's equivalent—including physically—brings his presents under the tree during the night of December 31 to January 1.
3. Easter cake with raisins, which took a long time to prepare. The other traditional Easter dish is Paskha, prepared with sweetened farmers cheese and candied fruit.
4. In Russia, parquet floors are washed with a cloth.
5. One of the suburbs that grew like mushrooms in the '60s and '70s.

6. "Limitchikis" are essential figures of the urban landscape, especially in Moscow where rationing was easier and where everybody wanted to live. Called to the capital for work, usually in construction, the "limitchik" obtained the famous "propiska," the right to reside in the capital, in exchange. Which did not save him from the scorn of born-and-bred Muscovites, who saw tens of thousands of people from the provinces install themselves in their kommunalki.
7. In a cramped area like a room in a kommunalka, the suitcase is a fundamental storage space. Filled with old clothes, shoes, lingerie, it is moreover always a presence in theater productions—countless—that all occur in the decor of a kommunalka.

## 17 How Thirty People Can Share an Apartment

1. Mikhail Kalinin (1875–1946) was the nominal head of state of the Soviet Union from 1919 to 1946 and one of the inner circle of party members around Stalin.
2. Arkady Raikin (1911–1987) was a Soviet stand-up comedian who led the school of Soviet and Russian humorists for about half a century. He was the only actor allowed to criticize during the '50s and '60s.
3. Russian word for Christmas tree.
4. Strictly speaking religion was not prohibited, but practicing meant lots of trouble with the authorities.
5. In 1931 the Cathedral of Christ the Savior was dynamited by order of Stalin. Before it was rebuilt after the fall of the Soviet Union, the Elokhovsky church in Moscow replaced it as the main Russian Orthodox worship center.
6. Russians eat very early as is often the case in the North.
7. The habit was still widespread in the beginning of the '90s and began to disappear with the onset of a market economy and the increase in energy costs. Gas was practically free in the USSR; the four burners of the stove stayed lit for entire days. They were used to heat the room, to light cigarettes.

## 18 The Gulag and the Roslovian Smell

1. Russian Social Democratic Worker's Party was a political party founded in 1898 which was split in 1903 into the Bolshevik Party and the Menshevik Party. The Mensheviks were finally suppressed after the 1917 Revolution.
2. Gosplan, or State Planning Committee, was responsible for economic planning in the Soviet Union.
3. Plekhanov University is one of the largest economic institutes of Russian higher education.

4. November 1926 was the defeat of the United Opposition, which was led by Lev Kamenev and Grigory Zinoviev.
5. Most of them, like Zinoviev and Trotsky, would be excluded from the Communist Party before the end of 1927. Trotsky was assassinated on Stalin's order in Mexico in 1940. The rest perished in the Great Terror of the 30s.
6. "Dom na Naberezhnoi" "The House on the Embankment" was a huge grey building opposite the Kremlin where all the dignitaries of the regime were housed. It became the title of a famous novel by Yuri Trifonov.
7. Financial autonomy, account balancing for businesses, in opposition to a totally centralized system under State control. The debate on the khozrashchet went on regularly in the USSR, until the Gorbachev period when it was adopted in the '80s.
8. Young Communists League where membership was practically obligatory in order to get into University.
9. A solitary cell in prison. Created after the Revolution, they were the first destination for communist "deviants" before being integrated into the jail system.
10. A prison in the basement of the KGB's headquarters where interrogations often took place.
11. Another Moscow prison.
12. Region located in the East European Plain of Russia.
13. Secret police.
14. City 122 miles south-east of Moscow.
15. The 20th Congress of the Communist Party of the Soviet Union (CPSU) is famous for Nikita Khrushchev's "Secret speech," which denounced the personality cult and dictatorship of Joseph Stalin.
16. Mikhail Tukhachevsky (1893–1937), Alexei Rykov (1881–1938), and Nikolai Bukharin (1888–1938) were some of the most prominent victims of Stalin's Great Purges.
17. Yves Montand (1921–1991). French actor and singer with leftist convictions who was popular in the Soviet Union.
18. In French, pink cherry trees and white apple trees.
19. Moskova is the river on which Moscow stands.
20. A species of fish—a ray.

## 19   Ballad of a Soldier

1. Grigory Chukrai (1921–2001). Prominent Soviet film director and screenwriter. Father of the director Pavel Chukrai. *Ballad of a Soldier* (1959), which he co-wrote and directed, is one of his most famous films.

2. Komsomolskaia Pravda is today a Russian tabloid newspaper. It was the All-Union Newspaper of the Soviet Union and an official organ of the Central Committee of the Komsomol between 1925 and 1991. The Komsomol was the youth wing of the Communist Party.
3. Aleksei Adzhubei (1924–1993). Prominent Soviet journalist during the Cold War era. He was married to the daughter of Nikita Khruschev.
4. Obshezhitie: a hostel basically for students or workers. A whole other facet of life in Russia and particularly in Moscow, as unbelievable as that of the Kommunalka.
5. In the USSR, black was the color of all ministerial vehicles, from simple Volgas to Chaika limousines or Zils. Things have changed as Russian ministers have become infatuated with western sedans.
6. Sergei Iutkevich (1904–1985). Soviet motion picture director and theorist.
7. Lev Kuleshov (1899–1970) Soviet film maker and film theorist.
8. Mikhail Romm (1901–1971). Soviet film director.
9. Mark Donskoi (1901–1981). Soviet film director. He won the Stalin prize for his *Gorky Trilogy*.
10. Sergei Paradzhanov (1924–1990). Armenian film director and artist and one of the most important film directors of his generation. He was arrested in 1973 on trumped-up charges of rape, homosexuality, and bribery. He was imprisoned for four years, and could not resume directing until the mid-1980s. He is well-known for his film *The Color of Pomegranates* (a.k.a. *Sayat Nova*) (1968) and *Shadows of Forgotten Ancestors* (1964).
11. Mosfilm, established in November 1923, was one of the largest film studios in Europe, located Moscow.
12. Ivan Pyriev (1901–1968). Soviet film director. He was the recepient of six Stalin Prizes and served as the director of Mosfilm Studio from 1954–1957.
13. Naum Naumov-Strazh (1898–1957). Soviet cinematographer from Kronstadt, near St. Petersburg. *We Are From Kronstadt* is one of his better-known films.
14. Ekaterina Furtseva (1910–1974). Influential woman in Soviet politics and the first woman to be admitted into the Politburo. She sided with Nikita Khruschev in de-Stalinization.

## 20  Lenins, Nothing But Lenins

1. Alexander Kolchak (1874–1920). Russian naval commander and head of the anti-Communist white forces during the Russian Civil War.
2. Important sum for the era. Up until 1991 and the end of the USSR, 300 rubles was a good monthly salary and a car cost 9,000 rubles. The prices remained unchanged until the fall of the Soviet Union.

3. Soviet Automobile brand. At that time it was very difficult to have a car, even a basic one like the Moskvitch, not only because of the price but also the waiting list.
4. There also, like everything else, "the plan" held sway.
5. The official news agency of the Soviet government.
6. The "Khudsoviet", or "Artistic Soviet", essentially had the role of political censor, rather than artistic.
7. Pyotr Sysoev. Art critic and hard-line advocate of Soviet Realism.
8. Anastas Mikoyan (1895–1978). Soviet statesman during the Stalin and Khruschev years.
9. Sverdlovsk was the Soviet name from 1924 to 1991 for the city Ekaterinburg in the Urals, where Tsar Nicholas II and his family were executed in 1918.

## 21   Dissidence

1. City in western Russia 116 miles southwest of Moscow.
2. A building with individual apartments constructed under Khrushchev who was aware of the kommunalka dramas. In the large cities, the number of Soviets living in communal apartments was around 70 percent, the number has been at a decreasing percentage ever since. In Moscow however, it was around 25 percent (1.7 million people) and significantly larger in St. Petersburg in the spring of 1999. In 2010, very few kommunalki remain in Moscow, more in St. Petersburg.
3. "Pobeda" i.e., "victory," rounded car typical of the Stalin era.
4. Chief of the KGB under Mikhail Gorbachev and one of the principal instigators of the August 1991 putsch in Moscow.
5. Lenin's wife. Others see the Virgin Mary.
6. Larisa Bogoraz (1929–2004). One of the most important dissidents in the Soviet Union, she became well-known when, on August 25, 1968, she organized a protest in Red Square against the invasion of Czechoslovakia.
7. The decrees and circulars regarding adjoining rooms: when rooms measure less than x square meters [...] where a couple, parents, and children of the same sex as the parents can live together. Larissa Daniel's son could not be registered in a room, which adjoined that of his mother, because his father no longer resided there...the Kafkaesque world of Soviet administration is unfathomable.
8. A distant northern suburb of Moscow.
9. Magic paper: magic drawing board i.e., erasable board. In Soviet times it was called "sputnik disidenta," or "the dissident's companion."
10. Literally: "that washes out"—also magic drawing board.

## 22    The Passageway Room

1. Capital of Azerbaijan, a former Soviet republic in the Caucasus, which became independent in 1991.
2. Nikita Mikhalkov (b. 1945). Soviet and Russian film director, producer, and actor, best known for his Academy-Award winning film *Burnt By The Sun* (1994).
3. Application decrees and circulars.
4. A model factory where production numbers were under particular scrutiny.
5. Workers who were late even by ten minutes could incur criminal proceedings, and, under Stalin, even a camp sentence.

## 23    The Prostitute

1. The Parasite Law was a decree issued in 1961 entitled, "on strengthening the struggle with persons avoiding socially useful work and leading an anti-social, parasitic way of life," which unofficially targeted artists and non-office, non-factory working individuals.
2. Even more so than mice, cockroaches were the plague of communal apartments where the kitchens were especially filthy. The garbage bins often aggravated the situation.
3. The Finnish War was fought between Sweden and Russia from 1808 to 1809. As a result of the war, Finland separated from Sweden and became an autonomous part of Russia.
4. In fact, officially prostitution did not exist.
5. A fish store where the deals where as intense as at the butchers. Certain fish disappeared from fish stores for decades, in particular salmon and trout, that were very sought after. They were generally sold, like meat, "under the counter" at a much higher rate than the paltry price set by the state.

## 24    The French Lover

1. Former capital of the Soviet Republic of Kazakhstan, which became an independent state in 1991. In 1997 the city lost its status to Astana.
2. Vladimir Vysotsky (1938–1980). Iconic Soviet Russian singer, songwriter, poet, and actor whose career had an immense effect on Russian culture. Marina Vlady, a French actress of Russian descent, became his third wife in 1969. He died at 42.
3. The sham marriage was a classic solution to get a "propiska." But often even "real" marriages were contracted by the nonresident spouse for the same reasons.

## 25 Masha L. and the Spirit of the Kommunalka

1. Alexei Kosygin (1904–1980). Soviet statesman and chairman of the Council of Ministers from 1964 to 1980.
2. A neighborhood in central Moscow, not far from the circular boulevard where there are three train stations.
3. Cooperative in Soviet lingo means "private." At the end of the '80s, cooperatives were the first stirrings of private enterprise; cooperative apartments were also private property and did not belong to the state.

## 26 The English Girl and the Blackmarketeer

1. A medium-rate Moscow hotel built by the French at the time of Olympic games in 1980, well-known for black-marketeering.
2. Diminutive for Dmitry.
3. Foreign currency stores, reserved for foreigners. For a long time, they only sold souvenirs: caviar at "regular" prices, furs, then with the start of "joint ventures" in the beginning of the '90s, Western food products appeared in them. The name "Beriozka," literally, birch tree, which had been used for some time, from then on became obsolete.
4. Accurate, judging from different facts and from many stories collected for this work. Axes have been used for a long time to cut wood in winter, and doubtless have remained in the houses ever since.
5. Sealed doors were common in communal apartments for all sorts of less macabre reasons but always linked to someone's disappearance. One element that contributed to the tenseness of the kommunalka's atmosphere.

## 27 An Officer in the Strategic Nuclear Forces

1. Sea port in the extreme northwestern part of Russia, on the Kola Bay, not far from Russia's borders with Norway and Finland. Its satellite Severomorsk is an important base for the Russian navy, especially for their nuclear submarines.
2. A fat shoemaker's needle, which is used to make holes in leather.
3. Zampolit: a typical Soviet abbreviation of "Zamestitel Politichevskovo Otdela" an assistant in the political department.
4. A Russian port on the Black Sea.
5. A lot of Russians, mainly older people, spend many months at their dachas, which can either be tiny houses without running water or splendid wooden residences with porches. They make the most of it by seeding and planting;

the dacha's yield makes up a good portion of vegetables and berries that are preserved and eaten during the winter.
6. All Russian houses are equipped with these huge jars that are used mainly to preserve tomatoes.

## 28   From Putsch to Putsch

1. The Russian White House is a government building in Moscow and the symbol of the 1991 resistance to the failed coup attempt. It was subsequently shelled by Yeltsin's troops in 1993 after the dissolution of the parliament.
2. Alexander Rutskoi (b. 1947) and Ruslan Khasbulatov (b. 1942) tried and failed to lead a resistance to Boris Yeltsin during the 1993 constitutional crisis.
3. The capital of Lithuania, a former Soviet Republic, which was the first state to announce its secession from the Soviet Union in March 1990 and subsequently led the fight for independence from Moscow in the early 1990s. In January 1991 Moscow sent in troops, an act that culminated in the attack on the State Radio and Television building, killing at least 14 civilians.

## 30   Two Sisters through History

1. Named after the director Oleg Tabakov (b. 1935), one of the founding fathers of contemporary Russian theater. Several notable Russian actors studied with him, including Vladimir Mashkov (b. 1963).